RECONCILIATION:

Celebrating God's Healing Forgiveness

RECONCILIATION:
Celebrating God's Healing Forgiveness

Rev. Chris Aridas

IMAGE BOOKS
A Division of Doubleday & Company, Inc.
Garden City, New York
1987

Library of Congress Cataloging-in-Publication Data

Aridas, Chris, 1947–
   Reconciliation: celebrating God's healing forgiveness.

   1. Penance. 2. Reconciliation—Religious aspects—
Catholic Church. 3. Catholic Church—Doctrines.
I. Title.
BX2260.A86 1987   265'.6   87-5344
ISBN 0-385-24022-8 (pbk.)

The English translation of the prayers of the penitent from the *Rite of Penance* (Second Edition) © 1974, International Committee on English in the Liturgy, Inc. (ICEL); the English translation of *Rite of Penance: Appendix III: Form of Examination of Conscience* © 1975, ICEL. All rights reserved.

Examination of Conscience #2, Chapter Six from *DISCERNMENT: Seeking God in Every Situation* published by Living Flame Press, Copyright © 1981 by Chris Aridas (Third Printing, 1983). Used by permission.

Scriptural Citations from The New Jerusalem Bible
Copyright © 1985 by Darton, Longman & Todd, Ltd.
and Doubleday & Company, Inc.
Used by permission of the publishers.

ISBN 0-385-24022-8
Library of Congress Catalog Card Number:
Copyright © 1987 by Chris Aridas

Dedicated to my brother,
Robert

Contents

Acknowledgments

One cannot experience the fullness of Church alone. Others are needed lest the experience be narrow and shallow, parochial and self-centered. As with Church, so it can be with writing a book. If an individual takes it upon himself/herself to "go it alone," the odds are that failure is a guaranteed by-product. Realizing that communicating the theme of this book would be difficult enough, I knew from the beginning that help would be needed. And so, from the very outset, I sought such help. It is these helpers whom I wish to thank now.

First, my office staff who willingly picked up the loose ends of office work as I tied together the loose ends of the manuscript. To Diane, Sr. Rep, Martha, Steve, and John, a sincere thank you. In addition, those with whom I live were most supportive and generous, especially John Gorman, my pastor, who always relinquished computer time so I could work at my convenience. Friends such as Steve, Jim, and Greg, without whom I would know very little about reconciliation, added to the manuscript in ways that cannot be expressed. My professor, the Reverend Stephen Babos, S.J., must also be singled out for the many times he reviewed the manuscript, offering concrete assistance, direction, and encouragement. Finally, the many people with whom I have had the privilege of celebrating the Sacrament of Reconciliation. Their faith and openness to God's Spirit have taught me more than books could ever teach. To them a heartfelt "Thank you."

Preface

"One of the Pharisees invited him to a meal. When he arrived at the Pharisee's house and took his place at table, a woman came in, who had a bad name in town. She had heard he was dining with the Pharisee and had brought with her an alabaster jar of ointment. She waited behind him at his feet, weeping, and her tears fell on his feet, and she wiped them away with her hair; then she covered his feet with kisses and anointed them with the ointment.

"When the Pharisee who had invited him saw this, he said to himself, 'If this man were a prophet, he would know who this woman is and what sort of person it is who is touching him and what a bad name she has.' Then Jesus took him up and said, 'Simon, I have something to say to you.' He replied, 'Say on, Master.' 'There was once a creditor who had two men in his debt; one owed him five hundred denarii, the other fifty. They were unable to pay, so he let them both off. Which of them will love him more?' Simon answered, 'The one who was let off more, I suppose.' Jesus said, 'You are right.'

"Then he turned to the woman and said to Si-

mon, 'You see this woman? I came into your house,
and you poured no water over my feet, but she has
poured out her tears over my feet and wiped them
away with her hair. You gave me no kiss, but she
has been covering my feet with kisses ever since I
came in. You did not anoint my head with oil, but
she has anointed my feet with ointment. For this
reason I tell you that her sins, many as they are,
have been forgiven her, because she has shown such
great love. It is someone who is forgiven little who
shows little love.' Then he said to her, 'Your sins
are forgiven.' " (Lk 7:36–48)

When were the woman's sins forgiven? The question is alarming in its implications. When was the
woman forgiven: when Jesus said the words "Your
sins are forgiven"; when the woman wept at Jesus'
feet; when she dried his feet with her hair; when she
kissed him; when she poured the ointment? When
were her sins forgiven?

Perhaps you felt it happened when Jesus said the
words "Your sins are forgiven." On the other hand,
the passage does say, "For this reason I tell you
that her sins, many as they are, *have been forgiven*
her . . ." Maybe her sins were always forgiven and
it really did not matter whether or not she came to
Jesus. More than likely you couldn't quite pin it
down, though the text seems to imply that a process
was involved—a process beginning with love offered and ending with love received and celebrated.

The purpose of this book is to help the reader

answer such a question with confidence, faith, and hope in the Lord's mercy and love. Beginning with a pictorial definition, we proceed to Part One, with chapter 1 offering a brief history of the Church's experience of reconciliation. This will allow us to see our roots as a believing community.

In chapter 2, the first steps in developing a theology of reconciliation will be taken. This journey will begin with a reflection on a basic tenet of our faith, God as triune. Such an approach will provide a common language which can be used to probe the topic at hand. Having explained this language, it will be applied to the story of the Fall in Genesis. This will lead us into a discussion on the reality of sin—a truth which must be recognized if we are to grasp a balanced understanding of reconciliation. Concluding this chapter is the social dimension of reconciliation. This is presented so that the reader can see, within our contemporary age, how the Lord continues to reconcile, and what implications spring from the experience of reconciliation. Those seeking to pursue the academic and theological basis of these chapters should refer to the notes in the back of the book.

In chapter 3, the Sacrament of Reconciliation, as it is presented in the *Rite of Penance* (1973), will be described. This chapter will offer the reader an opportunity to prepare himself/herself for the celebration of the sacrament by reviewing the dynamic involved in the celebration itself. Finally, chapter 4 will present a pastoral overview, including some

thoughts concerning the experience of God's forgiveness through channels other than the Sacrament of Reconciliation.

In order to assist the reader on a practical level,
Part Two offers several "hands on" experiences.
Chapter 5 presents selected scripture references so
the penitent might be encouraged by God's promises of mercy. Chapter 6, a "how to" chapter, offers
explanatory material on the examination of conscience, sample Prayers of the Penitent (Acts of
Contrition), and an example of the celebration itself. This is followed by a brief description of Inner
Healing Prayer in chapter 7. Finally, in chapter 8,
some questions one might have regarding a previous understanding of reconciliation are examined.

Before beginning, please note the use of the
phrases "sacrament of penance" or "sacrament of
reconciliation" in the historical treatment of the
topic. For ease of communication, the term "sacrament of penance" will be used even when referring
to the historical time preceding Peter Lombard's
classification and explanation of the seven effica-
cious signs, traditionally known as the seven sacraments of the Church. Use of the term is not meant
to imply a similarity with our contemporary experience of the sacrament. The context of the sentence
will usually suffice for understanding the correct
meaning of the term. Use of the term "sacrament of
reconciliation," however, is meant to indicate the
rite as the Church now celebrates it, according to
its promulgation in 1973.

With trust in the guiding power of God's spirit, my hope and prayer is that you will come to know the breadth and depth of God's love given freely to those who seek, that you will come to know communion with the Lord who died and rose for all, and, being convinced of his love, you will be moved to turn to him anew.

Introduction

DEFINITION

Definitions are usually boring—often linking a series of technical words which fail to communicate the real meaning of the word in question. This was true for me when inspecting the meaning of the word reconciliation. Webster's Dictionary gave the standard synonyms: make friendly again; settle a quarrel; compose a difference; bring into harmony; make someone content. However, a recent event in my life made one definition come alive.

It was not suppose to rain. The signs in the sky said sailor's delight. There was little reason that we should not continue on the new route which would lead us to the Gulf of Mexico. Besides, we had already spent several days canoeing through the maze of waterways which make up the Everglades. Though interesting beyond expectation, I still wanted to see the Gulf of Mexico. It might be the only chance I would ever get.

The canoe was an old wooden warhorse type of vessel. Joe had found it in a garage sale. He decided, on the spur of the moment, that it was just what was needed. Besides, it cost a mere hundred dollars. I remember when I first saw it, suspended from his garage beams. I was a bit skeptical, but he assured me that the canoe was truly seaworthy. All it needed was some sprucing up. Hesitantly I agreed. We'd clean it up and take the canoe with us for a two-week trip through the Florida Everglades. Little did I realize what the future held.

The storm hit rather suddenly. It seemed as if the clouds marched in within minutes. There was little or no warning. Within the space of a breath held momentarily, we were tossed from crest to crest like a cork on the surf. The clouds darkened the skies, and the rains pelted us with hot stings of impact. I don't know how we managed; yet the canoe remained afloat, and continued to respond to our steering commands. Finally we got to the island at the mouth of the river. It was only a few hundred yards away but it seemed farther than the longest journey. After dragging ourselves and the old, wooden canoe onto land, we had few options. The rain and the wind were too strong for the tent to be erected; we couldn't stay in the open, and there were no trees to provide shelter. As if we had received the same message simultaneously, we quickly secured the canoe on its side and found protection underneath its heavy hull. It was cramped, but dry—our only protection from the elements until the storm passed. As if to prove that choices are never made in a vacuum, a raccoon, huddling under the bow of the canoe, joined us for the night.

As quickly as it had come, the storm blew away, leaving (so I was told later) a wake of destruction along the coast. Though a bit chilled, we were safe, still not sure what had hit us. All I knew was that the canoe had not leaked or split apart during the time on the Gulf. I still don't know who made the canoe, but I am very grateful.

It was this experience which helped me understand the power of the word reconciliation. You see, another definition of the word comes from shipbuilding, and it means "to join evenly with another." This, of course, refers to the joints of the vessel itself. They must be joined evenly so they don't leak; they must be joined evenly so they appear as one unit although they are made of several; they must be joined evenly so they can withstand the storms which will be encountered. That's reconciliation in a pictorial way: it's our being joined "evenly" to God although we are not "even" in nature or power; it's our being joined "evenly" to God although there is an infinite distance between us; it's our being joined "evenly" to God as his adopted children although time and time again we have failed to believe. Finally, it is our being joined "evenly" to one another, because we have been joined "evenly" to God through Christ in the Spirit. But here I am a bit ahead of myself, so let's backtrack for a moment.

PART ONE

1 / A Historical Overview

PRESENT-DAY EXPERIENCE

Many adult Catholics continue to hold a limited understanding of the Sacrament of Reconciliation. Having "completed" their religious training by receiving the Sacrament of Confirmation, they try to live an adult life empowered by an adolescent understanding of the sacrament. Because of this, they remain rooted in a past experience of fear, "dark confessional boxes," memorized acts of contrition, lists of sins, etc. Fortunately, this is changing. The Church's understanding and celebration of the sacrament is deepening, and, in the process, is being adapted to our contemporary experience.

Unfortunately, what the official Church teaches and what is heard in the pews are often worlds apart. Those responsible for catechizing our adult community are often hampered by the same barriers and preconceived notions under which the believing community labors. Although the new Rite of Penance has been promulgated since 1973, many Catholic parishes remain stymied as to the best way to inaugurate the new ritual within a pastoral setting. In many cases, therefore, the old ritual is often the one used, thereby delaying the community's experience of the Church's contemporary perception and celebration of reconciliation.

Because of this, the people have remained misinformed and uninformed regarding the Church's understanding and celebration of the sacrament. It's no wonder that our adult community remains locked in an adolescent experience of reconciliation. Rome, of course, was not built in a day, and the same holds true for the Sacrament of Reconciliation. Although it has been officially revised, it will take many generations for the experience to filter down to all the faithful. A brief history of the sacrament itself will help us understand the process involved. It will also enable us to see how the Church struggles to respond to the Spirit's prompting in making revisions, changes, and adaptations based on the experience of the people of God.

THE HISTORY

In beginning our inspection of the historical development of the celebration of reconciliation throughout the ages, one must remember that growth is organic in nature, not cumulative. Unlike a beaver who builds a dam with methodical certainty stick by stick, each piece holding the others (and the dam) in place, the way that God's people have grown in celebrating reconciliation is more like a seed unfolding gradually as it becomes united to the earth which holds it. Who, looking at a seed, could imagine that a tree or a flower is "contained" within? The same is true with reconciliation. Who, when looking at Israel's awareness of God's Spirit in creation and in the exodus, would ever dream that covenant, redemption, cross, and resurrection lie within?

The fact that a seed develops through many stages as it unlocks the tree within, and that the tree continues to develop, never remaining static, gives us a further insight into the developing process of celebrating God's forgiveness. In fact, the very diversity that has emerged points to the growing and living awareness of the Spirit that is present in the created order. This fact is seen with unparalleled clarity when studying the history of salvation among God's people in the Old and New Testaments. There, local customs, national traditions, historical situations, etc., all added to the aliveness of the Spirit's presence within the people God called his own.

This history of dynamic growth and development is meant to encourage us even today as the Church encounters a drastic decline in the celebration of reconciliation. Perhaps this decline is merely signaling a new awareness of ways to respond to the reconciling love shown through the Father's only Son, Jesus.[1] This would be apparent if we inspected the varying images of God that have inspired the People of God's response to the Father through the ages. When the Old Testament people "saw" their

God in terms of cultic deity, nature God, warrior, etc., their experience and response to the invitation of reconciliation and forgiveness took on a particular form and structure, set off by particular laws and commands. This is articulated by the high priority of the Ten Commandments within the life of the Old Testament people. When the image of God became enfleshed in Jesus of Nazareth, the Good Shepherd, the Suffering Servant, the celebration of reconciliation took on a different texture, one that emphasized mercy, love, forgiveness. Here the Beatitudes became the norm to follow.

Throughout the history of the Church these images continued to exert an influence on the community's response to God's call, "Come back to me." The early Church, ever aware that it was the body of Christ, saw the communal and social dimension of reconciliation. The structure that developed during that time emphasized this communal understanding of forgiveness. For them, it was not a matter of hurting God, but of wounding the body of Christ present in the Church. Reconciliation, therefore, had to be structured in such a way that the Christian community present could celebrate the healing of the member within its very body. The Middle Ages, however, highlighted God's splendor, majesty, kingship. This God was unapproachable, distant, omnipotent. Here, reconciliation took root in structures which emphasized judgment, atonement, reparation, ransom. In other eras when the presence of God was portrayed with a more inti-

mate visage, the structures that surrounded reconciliation became more intimate, such as those developing today. Now face-to-face confession and
penance services filled with sensing experiences
characterize such an image of God.

Scriptural Background

Throughout the Old Testament, covenanted
communion with God was considered the only
source of life. A break or a rupture in that communion was death itself. In the words of Deuteronomy: "I am offering you life or death, blessing or
curse. Choose life, then, so that you and your de-
scendants may live, in the love of Yahweh your
God, obeying his voice, holding fast to him; for in
this your life consists . . ." (Dt 30:19–20). Should
a break occur, only God's initiation could restore
the person back to the covenanted relationship
promised Abraham. This is seen throughout the
prophetic period when men and women, speaking
the Lord's mind, called the people back to the
source of life and blessing, back to a relationship
with the Lord.

Despite many "breaks" in that relationship, the
people of Israel came to understand that God's love
for them was eternal, and that he would continually
forgive them "for the sake of his name." To celebrate this reality, penitential practices abounded:
fasting, weeping, mourning, the wearing of penitential garb such as sackcloth (Jl 1–2); prayers for

mercy (Lm 5; Ps 51, 60, 74, 79) and sacrifices of expiation were offered (Lv 1–7); intercessions of a community leader were also sought (Ex 32:30; Jr 14). Such practices, however, were not enough. Ritual *qua* ritual was insufficient. Change of heart was needed—a change which only God could initiate as stated in Ps 51:10: "God, create in me a clean heart, renew within me a resolute spirit." The new heart, the resolute spirit for which the psalmist prayed, was realized in the life-death-resurrection of Jesus, bearer of the new covenant in New Testament times.

A hallmark of New Testament experience is the constant reiteration that God's initiative, realized in the dying and rising of Jesus, is pure gift offered by God who "wanted all fullness to be found in him [Jesus] and through him to reconcile all things to him" (Col 1:19). This initiative fills us "with exultant trust in God, through our Lord Jesus Christ, through whom we have already gained our reconciliation" (Rm 5:11).

For the New Testament believer, therefore, Jesus alone is the one who restores us to life giving communion in the power of the Spirit; Jesus alone is the one whose life in our midst provided the possibility of divine restoration, once and for all; Jesus alone is the one who completes the original plan of God the Father by accepting in his own flesh the unbreakable link of sonship offered through the Spirit, allowing all who abide in him to be linked forever to the Father as adopted children. The concrete impli-

cations of this reality were not lost on St. Paul
when he described God's purpose, that is, the unity
that can now exist among all people: "to create a
single New Man out of the two of them [Jew and
Gentile], and through the cross, to reconcile them
both to God in one Body" (Ep 2:15–16). The far-
reaching consequences of this unity are made even
clearer in 2 Co 5:18–21 when believers are exhorted
to proclaim the reconciliation which takes place
through Jesus Christ.

In order to celebrate the fact of reconciliation,
various practices arose throughout New Testament
communities.[2] There was the "one on one" ministry
which took the shape of fraternal correction, prayer
for, and confession to one another (Mt 18:15–20).
Practical examples of this exhortation abound. For
example, in Galatians 6:1–2 Paul urges: ". . . even
if one of you is caught doing something wrong,
those of you who are spiritual should set that person right in a spirit of gentleness; and watch yourselves that you are not put to the test in the same
way." Matthew also reminds the Christian that the
proper attitude is to seek reconciliation first and
foremost, even to leaving your offering there before
the altar, going to be reconciled first, and then coming back to present your offering (cf. Mt 5:23–24).

Another form which developed involved the entire community. This took place only when the
"one on one" ministry did not bear fruit. This form
involved a group of people urging reconciliation. If
that did not bring results, the sinner was to be ex-

pelled from the community itself (1 Co 5:1–5). However, after a period of separation, the community is to offer "forgiveness and encouragement" lest the sinner "break down from so much misery" (2 Co 2:5–11). Encouraged in this way, the sinner can enter again the full expression of communion within the body.

Please note that the texts of the New Testament do not identify the sacrament of penance as we experience it today. Traditionally, John 20:23—"Receive the Holy Spirit. If you forgive anyone's sins, they are forgiven; if you retain anyone's sins, they are retained"—has been held as the "institution" of the sacrament by Jesus. New Testament scholars, however, do not locate such an "event" within the above scriptural reference. Rather, they see in the text the community's power to "isolate, repel, and negate evil and sin" worked out differently within individual church communities, each specifying "both the manner and agency of its exercise."[3] This is not to say that the sacrament as we experience it today does not stem from Christ. On the contrary, it shows an organic process at work as the community, led by the Spirit, celebrates God's forgiveness in different ways, reflecting the diverse aspects present within the treasury of abounding grace. John's text, for example, highlights the community's participation and power in the reconciliation process. If the community were to be like Christ, it had to acknowledge its power to isolate or include, to repel

or embrace, to negate or affirm a person and his/
her relationship to the body.

Though forms differed, the community was certain of a basic truth: anyone who sinned could be
forgiven through the ministry of the Church.[4] The
seed of that conviction was rooted in Christ's victory over sin, and the power he handed on to his
"ambassadors of reconciliation": to Peter
(Mt 16:19) when he received the keys of the kingdom, and to the disciples (Mt 18:18) when they are
reminded of the power they hold over one another
in fraternal correction. Nevertheless, no well-deter-
mined structure existed within which this could occur. Sacred signs and gestures needed to develop.

The First Six Centuries

In the Christian community, there was always a
close relationship between the evolving understanding of sin and the celebration of the sacrament of
penance. (Please remember, I am using the term
"sacrament of penance," realizing it is anachronis-
tic before the twelfth century.) The question before
the Church during these early centuries was not
whether God could forgive sins after baptism, but
whether the Church could or should. For the longest time there was a great deal of hesitancy on the
part of the Church to offer a second baptism experience to the believer. This, despite the primary Gospel focus of Christ's victory over sin.

One must not be too harsh with our forebears,

however. Realize that there was a tension between the Church's experience of Matthew 18:22, which spoke of forgiving seventy times seven, and Romans 6:2, which stated with equal certainty, "We have died to sin; how could we go on living in it?" In addition, one must remember that the question of committing serious sin after one was baptized was far from the initial experience of the early community. Moved with unparalleled fervor and faith, our forebears embraced the demands of Christian life with passionate love. Nothing would stand in the way of their reaching for the eternal crown of glory which would soon be theirs, when Jesus returned in glory. Furthermore, Christianity was an adult reality, accepted by adults as adults, and lived within the context of a strong, adult support group known as the community of believers.

Still, where there are humans, there are sinners. Tertullian, for example, before his conversion to Montanism, considered that the Church's power to forgive sins after baptism was "a second plank after shipwreck." The *Shepherd of Hermas* (c. 140), steering a course between rigorism and complete laxity, also allowed for forgiveness to be granted when grave sins were involved. Such an experience, however, could occur only once in a person's lifetime. If grave sin were not involved, which was decided by the bishop's discretion and judgment, the normal forms of mortification were used to celebrate forgiveness, namely fasting, almsgiving, prayers, etc.

By the third century, three persecutions precipitated a more definite decision on the part of the believing community. These persecutions—Decius (250–51), Gallus (253), and Valerian (257–58)—rocked the Church with intensity, bringing many to martyrdom, and, unfortunately, many to apostasy. The Church, therefore, had to determine if and how the apostates might be reintegrated into the community of believers. Finally, led by St. Cyprian and Pope Cornelius at the Council of Carthage (251), it was decided that mercy and favor would be granted those who denied the faith during the persecution. This offer was to be received only once.

Immediately a dispute arose. A Roman priest, Novatianus, challenged the decision, thereby setting the scene for an eventual schism. To external appearances, severity versus clemency seemed to be at stake: should the Church forgive sins held by some to be unforgivable—apostasy, murder, adultery?[5] Historically, however, Novatianus' jealousy at not being chosen Bishop of Rome over Cornelius may have had a lot to do with his defending the pure ideals of the Gospel! By the fourth century, after many years of disagreement, a canonical or ecclesiastical structure emerged for the forgiveness of sins after baptism.

"Public Penance"

The experience of penance arising around the fourth century went under many titles. Ecclesiastical or canonical penance indicated the Church's active role in shaping the celebration. Ancient or solemn penance indicated the gravity and the grandeur of the celebration itself. The term most common among the people, however, was "public penance," a true misnomer since the phrase usually led an individual to infer that the penitent's sins were confessed "publicly," a practice condemned by Pope Leo I in 249.

Perhaps the most important aspect in this stage of development was its emphasis on the process involved in reconciliation, a process pictured within the framework of ongoing conversion.[6] Several distinct stages were employed. First, the penitent was enrolled in the Order of Penitents. This was a community event beginning with the sinner's confession of sins to the bishop, who alone decided whether or not the sins were grave enough to warrant enrollment in the penitential order. Note that the confession was made to the bishop, not to the community per se. Once enrolled into the Order of Penitents, the community responded in praise of God who had led the sinner to receive the grace of repentance.

It was at this time that the penitent was "excommunicated," that is, removed from the main body of believers, thereby completing the break initiated by sin.[7] No longer would the penitent receive the Eucharist since he/she was no longer part of the body's wholeness or holiness. Though cut off from the Eucharist, the person still remained God's child, and so was encouraged to seek nourishment (and correction) through the Liturgy of the Word. Relegated to the back of the Church, the "excommunicated" penitent, with tears, prayers, and prostrations, would greet the community as the believers gathered for the eucharistic assembly. In response, the people would pray for and with the penitent, thereby joining their penance with his/hers. The bishop too would offer prayers continuously, often gathering with others in prayer over the penitent.

There were, of course, public acts of penance. These actions, the length and type of which were determined by the bishop, would often extend for many years, or even a lifetime. It was the bishop who decided when repentance had truly ripened in the heart of the sinner; hence, it was the bishop who called the penitent back into unity with the eucharistic community. This was accomplished when the bishop, standing at the rear of the Church, offered some final prayers for the penitent, who, accompanied by the bishop or delegated assistant, was led back to his/her previous place among the faithful. By the fifth century, this part of the celebration took place on Holy Thursday.

Despite being reintegrated into the community, the penitent's life did not return to "normal." Once a penitent, always a penitent was the basic rule of thumb.[8] A variety of disciplines was often imposed upon the "born again" (for a second time) Christian. Exclusion from clerical orders, from military service, from holding public office were a few of the prohibitions imposed. Undoubtedly, the purpose of the entire penitential process was ongoing rehabilitation!

Personal Sin as Corporate Effect: The Body of Christ as One

This period in the Church's history was a time of insight and drama. It displayed the unshaken conviction and insight that a sinner could be forgiven through the ministry of the community.[9] In addition, it lived and breathed the drama of communal involvement within the process of the sinner's reconciliation, an involvement precipitated by the belief expressed in 1 Peter 1:15 quoting Leviticus 11:44: "Be yourselves holy in all your activity, after the model of the Holy One who calls us, since scripture says: 'Be holy, for I am holy.' "

The entire Church, therefore, was obliged to take an active part in the sinner's reconciliation with God, since the individual member's unity or rupture with God affected the community's holiness. It was not out of order, therefore, for the community to imitate Christ by placing itself at-one with the sinner in the hope that the sinner would become one again with the body. The sign that a unity with the body was indeed being effected came through the penitent's sincerity and faithfulness in performing the works of penance imposed by the bishop. These had to be fulfilled to the bishop's satisfaction before absolution, signifying the unity restored, could be given. Such an approach may upset our contemporary sensibilities, which are used to absolution being received before the penance is performed. The early Church, however, viewed the acts of penance as the sign of the penitent's willingness to experience again the grace and responsibilities of baptism, that is, the grace of living the life-style of Jesus within his body, the Church community.

Transition Period

By the end of the sixth century, the ancient or "public" penance of the early Church collapsed under its own weight. No longer embraced by the faithful, fewer and fewer people approached the bishop for enrollment in the Order of Penitents. Soon the sacrament became associated with death-bed reconciliation. It was, in fact, passing into oblivion even as it peaked.[10]

The reasons for its demise are sundry. First and foremost, Christianity itself was increasing in power and influence, despite the barbarian invasion. It was during this time, in fact, that the barbarians were being converted to the faith, thereby increasing the rank and file membership of the Church. As the numbers increased, the strength and conviction of believers, though sincere, began to fall a bit short of apostolic fervor and heroism. Even during times of persecution, traditionally a strong period in the

Church's life, the community found itself with more apostates than it knew how to handle.

Secondly, the faithful, being less involved in a ghetto type of community lifestyle, were no longer willing to accept the penitential consequences of the sacrament as it was celebrated in the ancient penance formulation. People did not desire to give up military service, or certain trades, for the sake of reconciliation. Though they loved the Kingdom, they were not quite willing to give up the world as of yet. In addition, as persecutions diminished, the solidarity of communal identity and resistance that usually emerged also waned, no longer operating as a binding force propelling the Church toward death-defying acts of belief. The former Empire was being converted. Christians, therefore, were no longer the minority struggling to maintain their identity. They were moving into the majority holding positions of power. It was here that they found their identity. Such a movement upward left little space for former penitential practices which would not allow for a second fall. Realizing the gravity of the situation, bishops hesitated to enroll anyone in the Order of Penitents who might not be able to withstand the temptations all around. This delay often extended to baptism itself.

Finally, the community sensed that Christ's imminent return was not as close as expected. This weakened the community's desire to pursue a rigid morality requiring heroic fervor since the Church's

earthly sojourn seemed to be taking a longer
route.[11]

The Seed Sprouts a New Shoot

During this time, the system of monasticism began to exert its influence throughout the Church.
Aside from the already known contribution of
"preserving" the arts of civilization from the barbarian onslaught, the monastic system also affected
the very core of spiritual growth among the
Church's members. This took place through the
practice of spiritual direction offered first to novices
under formation, but eventually to all the faithful.
In this system, each person would have a spiritual
companion or soul mate with whom he/she could
"confess" his/her sins. This form of "confession"
was not meant to be the sacrament of reconciliation
as we know it today. Rather, it was a simple exercise of sharing one's life's journey with another, so
the chosen companion could offer direction, encouragement, prayers, and discernment.

This very system touched deeply the heart of a
young monk named Patrick who, captured by barbarians, was taken to the Irish coast from where he
eventually escaped back to Gaul. There he fell under the influence of Bishop Germain d'Auxerre,
who promoted the monastic movement in Gaul.
Once Patrick was consecrated a bishop, he was sent
back to the land of his captivity in order to evangel-
ize the people there. Due to its familiarity, the story

of his success does not warrant repetition here. What does need exposition is the creative convergence initiated by monks such as Patrick, who joined their monastic experience of spiritual direction with a strategy for converting the barbarians.

Realizing that a tool was needed to facilitate bringing the Gospel's message to the heart of the barbarian tribes, the monks offered them God's forgiveness within the context of process conversion, that is, within the process of ongoing spiritual direction. Not dealing with the exceptional sinner who was reconciled to the Church through the solemn form of "public" penance, these evangelists, in an extraordinarily bold maneuver, offered God's mercy combined to the fairly recent structure of spiritual direction. This process would, theoretically, lead the barbarian gently and patiently on the road to holiness, through ongoing conscience formation.[12]

The Roots Go Deeper

The success which the monks experienced in Ireland was not to be limited to Patrick's adopted homeland. As the system of monasteries grew throughout the land, missionaries were sent back to the Continent to preach the Gospel. One such monk, Columban, returned to Gaul around A.D. 600 and began the process of reevangelizing the people. Naturally, he introduced the system of penance that had served well in Ireland. In addition, he

set up a monastic structure similar to the one experienced in Ireland. These eventually continued his
missionary thrust stretching their influence to
northern Italy and Switzerland.

Wherever there are different expressions of faith,
there are bound to be conflicts. It was no surprise,
therefore, that the new form of penance springing
from the Irish experience was not uniformly accepted. In 589, for example, the Third Council of
Toledo condemned the "detestable" practice, and
insisted that the Spanish Church remain rooted in
the ancient form of canonical penance. Less than
sixty years later, however, at a synod of French
bishops gathering at Chalon-sur-Saône (647–652),
the practice was deemed good for all, and "medi-
cine for the soul." Slowly the Irish influence was
felt even in Rome, where both forms existed in
tense juxtaposition. By the middle of the ninth century, a type of compromise arose: public penance
would be used for public and notorious sins, while
private penance would be used for secret sins.[13]

What Did It Look Like?

The characteristics of the Irish system of penance
were in vivid contradistinction to the ancient order.
There was no Order of Penitents or "one time
only" rule for reception of the sacrament. Reconciliation was open to all for an unlimited number of
times. There was no segregation from the community since the penitent did his/her penance in pri-

vate. In addition, he/she went to the priest, not the bishop, in order to confess and receive absolution. At first, absolution was held off until the imposed penance was completed. Eventually this gave way to expediency. Absolution was given immediately, since the monk hearing the confession was probably an itinerant priest who would not be back by the time the penance was completed.

In addition, the permanent "aftereffects" of penitential practices, such as withdrawing from military service, were no longer promulgated. Thus the penitent could receive absolution an innumerable number of times, based on the Irish practice of spiritual direction fostering the gradual process of conversion and growth. Finally, the emphasis on a few grave sins, such as murder, apostasy, or adultery, was no longer stressed. All and any sins could be confessed. Note, however, that the distinction between mortal and venial sins was made at a later date, and does not apply to this period in history.

In order to help the priest maintain the proportion between gravity of fault and severity of expiation, the use of penitential books, *liber poenitentialis,* grew. These were meant to help those who did not have the proper training or expertise in guiding the penitent toward a holy life. Originally they were geared toward rehabilitation, that is, the penance was meant to countermand the sin, thereby bringing about character reconstruction based on the correction of specific, personal defects. For this reason, "tariff" penance, a term taken from Celtic secular law to describe a penalty given to satisfy a crime, became a familiar nomenclature for the sacrament. This well-intentioned approach was meant to heal the sinner's soul, which was experiencing an interior illness due to sin. A quote from the *Penitential of Columban* (c. 600) will offer a clear example of the methodology: "The talkative person is to be sentenced to silence, the disturber to gentleness, the gluttonous to fasting . . . everyone shall suffer suitable penalties according to what he deserves, that the righteous may live righteously."[14] Later developments shifted the focus away from healing and moved it toward judgment and repayment. These books remained in vogue until around the twelfth century.

Relating to the rise of penitential books, a system of commutation, *arrea,* emerged. Through this, the penitent was able to commute his/her penance by giving it to another, by saying certain prayers, reading certain passages from scripture, and even by offering a donation. Needless to say, this led to many abuses. For example, the poor, for all practical purposes, were prevented from taking advantage of substitute penances, since they could neither read nor pay. One can imagine how very small a step it was to the buying and selling of indulgences which would plague the Church during a later age. Although this system of commutation may have been a way to foster again the sense of communal participation in the reconciliation process of the members, such a thrust never told hold.

The Growth Process Slows

By the eleventh century, a ritual of reconciliation was established, thereby canonizing the Irish experience of private penance.[15] This was further solidified in 1215 by Innocent III at the Fourth Lateran Council, which decreed: "Each member of the faithful of both sexes who has reached the age of discretion must confess his [her] sins at least once a year to his [her] own parish priest, and accomplish within the measure of his [her] means, the penance which is imposed."[16] Between this promulgation and the Council of Trent's restatement of the same, little changed in the Church's practice of penance. Although it was set in its external form, several important speculative questions arose which remain with us today.

Contritionists vs. Absolutionists

Without getting into details unsuited for this type of book, we can summarize the speculative questions that arose between the Fourth Lateran Council and the Council of Trent by looking at the relationship the penitent's actions (sorrow, confession, acts of penance) and the priest's action (absolution in the name of Christ in the Church) had on the forgiveness of sins. This might be expressed as the difference between the contritionists and the absolutionists.

On the contritionists' side of the controversy were Peter Abelard (d. 1142) and Peter Lombard (d. 1160), who held that sincere sorrow, motivated by the love of God, was the cause of forgiveness. Absolution was seen as a petitionary prayer rather than a juridical sign, except in the case of excommunication where a person was readmitted into the community of believers. For them, the priest's absolution was more a statement of the fact that forgiveness was already offered rather than being the formula through which forgiveness was granted.

The absolutionists, on the other hand, headed by Hugh (d. 1141) and Richard (d. 1173) of St. Victor (the Victorines' School of Thought) saw the priest's absolution as the proper use of Christ's power, known as the power of the keys, which was handed on to Peter and the apostles. According to this interpretation, the power of the keys was used to admit or exclude people from forgiveness, rather than admit or exclude people from the community, as in the case of excommunication and fraternal correction.

Using Aristotelian categories, Thomas Aquinas (d. 1274) tried to bring harmony back into the picture. He proposed that the individual's personal actions (sorrow, confession, acts of penance) were the matter for the sacrament; the ecclesial action (priest's absolution) was the form. Both were needed for the efficacy of the sacrament. One could not exist without the other. By taking this approach, Thomas was able to meld true conversion and contrition with the ecclesial action of absolution, thereby creating an integral experience. If, for example, true conversion and contrition were not in evidence, the priest would be expected to withhold absolution, since the sacrament could not work without both indicators being present. For Thomas, the sacramental process begins the very moment that conversion takes hold, leading the penitent toward God. Using the scripture story cited in the Preface, it is apparent that Thomas would not have highlighted one part of the process to the detriment of the other, but would maintain the entire flow as the experience of the sacrament.

Despite Thomas' sensible solution to the problem, the Victorine approach was picked up by Duns Scotus (d. 1308), who again repeated that absolution by a priest was required for forgiveness to take place. For Duns Scotus, the person's sorrow was meant to open one's heart to the forgiveness received through the priest's absolution. This effectively eliminated the practice of confessing to a lay person regardless of his/her charism for the ministry of spiritual direction, or his/her success in the ministry of guiding others toward holiness.[17] Duns Scotus did agree that sorrow motivated by perfect love of God (perfect contrition) would grant forgiveness. However, never being sure if one's contrition were perfect, he maintained that absolution was the surest way to be forgiven.

At this point in our historical survey, we can see that the catechetical reality of the Church fostered

Dun Scotus' view over Thomas', despite the fact that Thomas has been declared a Doctor of the Church. The repercussions of this historical twist of fate remain with us today. For example, the lack of community involvement with the reconciliation process has weakened our understanding of the body of Christ and the relationship of its members one to another. There is little sense, therefore, that one's confessing "to all the saints" includes the people who are present in our life as well as those who have received canonical status. In addition, one might easily fall into the trap of "cheap grace," which does not necessitate a sincere change of heart on the part of the penitent but relies on a vocal penance and the priest's absolution.

What About Now?

At this point, one might detect a similarity with our present-day experience of penance. Because of the protestations of the reformers who challenged the right of anyone, priest or not, to judge the conscience of another or to forgive sins in God's name, the Fathers of Trent advocated the absolutionist position. Done as a way of maintaining a "we're-right-you're-wrong" position in the dialectic of ideas, Trent maintained the judicial importance of the priest's absolution-granting role where he judged the penitent's disposition, imparted a fitting penance as a penalty for sin, and pronounced the judicial sentence in the form of absolution.[18] Such an approach seems, of course, to lessen the opportunity for the Church to proclaim God's mercy, or foster the community's role in the process of reconciliation, or promote the experience of thankfulness and praise which follows when forgiveness is accepted. An increasing number of today's scholars, however, hold the position expressed by Ladislas Orsy that Trent never intended to say that the priest was the judge inquisitor. Rather, the Council Fathers were trying to maintain that a priest held the highest judicial privilege, which was to show mercy and grant free pardon to those who were repentant.[19]

Trent also emphasized the need to confess the number of mortal sins committed. This is traditionally called "integral confession." Venial sins were not included. Although they could be "forgiven" through other penitential practices, the Council still advocated a type of "devotional confession" which was meant to strengthen the faithful on their journey. Such a procedure remains present today, having been advocated by Pope Pius XII in his encyclical *Mystici Corporis* (1943).

Historical Evaluation

In looking over the development that has taken place over the centuries, several possibilities can be recognized. One might assume that the initial experience of the Church as celebrated in the canonical or "public" form was indeed the only true expres-

sion of the sacrament. One might likewise assume
that the canonical form was only a prelude to the
"private" form which emerged from the sixth century on, and was advocated by the Council of Trent
(1551). Or one might assume that both forms,
though displaying certain limitations, were authen-
tic expressions and interpretations of the power
granted by the Lord to the apostles.[20]

Considering these possibilities, it seems more
than reasonable to embrace this latter conclusion in
light of the presentation made. Indeed, by accepting
such a position, we will be freed to look at the re-
cently promulgated *Rite of Penance* (1973) with its
historically conditioned forms and expressions. A
section from the Second Vatican Council's Docu-
ments points to the possibility of such a stance:
"For, as the centuries succeed one another, the
Church constantly moves forward toward the fullness of divine truth until the words of God reach
their complete fulfillment in her."[21]

2 / Toward a Theology of Reconciliation

THE THEOLOGY OF EXCHANGE

In order to examine the meaning, and life implications, of the Sacrament of Reconciliation, a framework is needed. Often called a methodology, the model or paradigm proposed is meant to provide the operating system which enables us to speak consistently and clearly about the topic at hand. Such a framework is not absolute, that is, mandating a point by point duplication or replica. Rather, it is a tool and a guide affording a perspective in the light of which the topic will make sense. The one chosen is Trinitarian in format, and will be referred to as the Theology of Exchange. Hopefully, this tool will help us probe the meaning of the topic in such a way that our minds will be opened to perceive what we experience in a new way, and to experience in a new way that which we may not yet perceive.

The Theological Paradigm

Through faith's revelation, the Christian community discovers within an ability to identify its Trinitarian experiences. For it is here that "the only cause of created things" is found. Here, in the goodness of the Creator, the one true God, he from whom this comes, "is the Trinity—to wit, the Father, and the Son begotten of the Father, and the Holy Spirit proceeding from the same Father, but one and the same Spirit of Father and Son."[1]

Whether our starting point be the unity of God, as seen in the opening sections of Augustine's *De Trinitate*, which speaks forcefully of the unity that is the Trinity—"The Father, the Son, and the Holy Spirit are of one and the same substance or essence" constituting "a divine unity of one and the same substance in an indivisible equality"[2]—or a later approach which emphasizes the necessary relationships and harmony, the flowing wholeness, which is meant for all that comes from God the Father, since all that is from him must in some way reflect his very being,[3] we have, in the Trinity, the Theology of Exchange paradigm affirming that "the Trinity is the acme of a truth that permeates all realms of being and consciousness and . . . links us together."[4]

In either approach, both the distinction of the Trinitarian Persons and the unity that is the Reality is maintained. St. Augustine, for example, emphasizing the Trinitarian unity, nevertheless, states clearly: "From the Scripture we learn with absolute certainty . . . and the eye of the mind perceives it with its unfailing perception, namely, that there is the Father, the Son, and the Holy Spirit, and the Son is not the same as the Father, and the Holy Spirit is not the same as the Father and the Son." For it was Christ, not the Trinity, who became man, the Father not the Trinity who spoke from the cloud, and the Spirit not the Trinity who descended as a dove.[5]

Bonaventure, on the other hand, begins with the distinctions. God the Father is the Source of all that is and all that is given.[6] And he who is Love has for all eternity expressed perfectly and completely all that he is or can be. This eternal Expression is the Word the Son, the Image of the Father.[7] This Word, who is eternally receiving in a passion of reciprocated giving all that the Father offers, receives ceaselessly and forever the Father's self gift (self-surrender), acknowledging that it is all from the Father. In doing so, the Word, in a sense, also acknowledges that his identity comes from the Father. His identity is Son. By accepting and acknowledging that this identity comes from the Father, the Son, in turn, gives everything back (self-surrender) to the Father. One might say, therefore, that the Father defines the Son and the Son defines the Father through their mutual and eternal giving, receiving-accepting, sharing-exchanging in the Spirit, that is, through their eternal self-surrender.[8]

The power of this exchange, which ceaselessly and eternally goes on in a loving dynamic, is the Spirit who participates completely and totally in the flow of wholeness which is God.[9] St. Bernard describes it as an eternal kiss; Rosemary Haughton calls it the passionate embrace of God; Dante:

> The uncreated Might which passeth speech,
> Gazing on His Begotten with the Love
> That breathes Itself eternally from each.
>
> *(Paradiso* X:1–3)

Applying this exchange to humanity, we can describe, with Augustine, this power as the Gift by which "we are borne upwards" and "ascend steps within the heart." For "by your fire, by your good fire, we glow with inward fire, and we go on, for we go upwards to 'the peace of Jerusalem' . . . There will goodwill find us a place, so that we may desire nothing further but to abide therein forever."[10] It is the Spirit that suggests to Augustine "the common love by which the Father and the Son mutually love each other." The Spirit who is the Son's mutual loving of the Father, and the Father's mutual loving of the Son in the eternal exchange that is Gift given and Gift received. It is this Holy Spirit "poured forth in our hearts, through which the whole Trinity dwells in us."[11]

In the exchange, therefore, the Spirit is "that perfect love which joins the Father and the Son and attaches us to them." He is the one diffused in our hearts who allows us to hold fast to the Eternal Image, the Father's Son.[12] He is the one who manifests to us the very grace of God, that is, "the adoption of His [Christ's] human nature into the divine."[13]

Without going into great detail, creation also continues this flowing wholeness within itself, and, in a unique way, within the person of Jesus who is the Expression of all that the Father can be in relation to the finite.[14] All that is created bears the imprint of the Trinitarian dynamic because it bears in its nature a relation to the uncreated Word, the Son, who is the total Expression of all that the Father is and can be.[15] Such a design allows us to peer at the unimaginable complexity, yet simplicity, of Reality exemplified in creation, particularly men and women. It allows us to conclude that all that is somehow mirrors the Trinitarian exchange of Father, Son, and Spirit: the flowing wholeness where distinctions remain while they are unified through the exchange of Love.[16] All must be one; all must be distinct.

These two approaches embrace the medieval fashion of speculation from the Trinity *ad intra*, that is, from the perspective of God's existence. Contemporary theologians, however, have discovered another gate into the mystery of the Triune God by beginning with the economic Trinity, that is, humanity's experience of God's saving work actualized in one Jesus of Nazareth, proclaimed Son of God by the early Church. In beginning here, with the faith experience of the early Church, our framework, the Theology of Exchange, is further enriched. Now, in viewing the Trinitarian paradigm within the economy of salvation, a descriptive synonym for the exchange is given, namely, self-surrender. This is to be equated with the experience called Spirit *ad intra;* and *ad extra*—as manifested in the life of Jesus of Nazareth. Love and self-surrender are one and the same within this framework.

In time and history, therefore, the eternal self-surrender of God is realized, expressed, and communicated in the person of Jesus of Nazareth. In his lifestyle of self-surrender, described in the Beatitudes, this Jesus of Nazareth, sanctified and consecrated by the Spirit as witness for God, lived, in the economy of salvation, the self-surrender which is characteristic of the eternal Trinity. Because the Word received flesh from Mary, human history became God's history; because God chose to live temporally through the self-emptying of Jesus, the self-surrender which is the eternal Trinitarian life *ad intra* became revealed as the very existential of all that is human.

The lifestyle of Jesus, described as self-surrender, is a type of exchange: Gift given by the Father's self-surrender (the gift of Sonship bestowed upon Jesus from the beginning), Gift received by the Son (whose own self-surrender was necessary to accept the Gift of the Father as the "authoring" of his identity as Son), and Gift shared by the Father and

Son (their mutual self-surrender expressed in the pouring out of the Spirit of sonship upon all).

By starting with the life of Jesus, men and women are shown as created not apart from but enveloped by the reality of God himself. In other words, humanity was not made in one way and then redesigned so the Divine might abide within. Rather, in the very existence of that which we call human, the Divine is. This possibility, called the supernatural existential in Rahnerian theology, is a key to understanding the total otherness of God, that is, his transcendence, as he abides in direct proportion to one's freely acknowledged and chosen response to that possibility. This is God's immanence. As such, God can be one with, and other than, his creation while offering the individual the creative possibility to choose his/her own identity and meaning within the context of ultimate meaning, namely, the eternal exchange of giving, accepting/receiving, sharing/exchanging characteristic of the Trinity *ad intra,* and characteristic of the Theology of Exchange.

Such an approach, at first glance, might seem to be the initial step on a useless journey into the world of philosophical razzle-dazzle. Upon reflection, however, its validity and importance become more apparent. For example, by starting with the economy of salvation, specifically the experience of Jesus of Nazareth, the transcendent is identified within human experience. In the life and death of Jesus we see one who encounters and chooses as true that which is beyond in the meaninglessness of hardship and pain. Is this not similar to our experience of being grasped in love by One who seems beyond the lover present to our human consciousness? There are many possible experiences of such transcendent moments wherein the reality of the Divine, present within and without, becomes visible in our knowing and choosing.[17] Traditionally called Love (in Jesus it would be called Divine Love Incarnate), in the Theology of Exchange it can also be named self-surrender, that is, the experience called Spirit which is the binding power and context of Trinitarian existence.

The purpose of highlighting self-surrender as the description of Trinitarian Spirit *ad intra* and *ad extra* is that love has become too common a word. It fails to draw forth the dual meaning of passion so vividly set forth by Rosemary Haughton throughout her book, *The Passionate God.*[18] The word self-surrender, however, seems to succeed in evoking a richer and deeper response.

In summary: The Father, though distinct from the Son, and the Son, distinct from the Father, and the Spirit, distinct from either, are one and same—existing harmoniously together, unified in a passionate embrace of self-surrender which is Love. Distinct, but the same One. That is the Trinity.

Made to Love

Seen from the Theology of Exchange presented thus far, it is clear that God's desire is to unite himself with his creation. In particular, men and women are to be one with him, and he one with them. This is accomplished "in the Spirit" which is the self-surrender of Father and Son within creation. It is a gift freely given—unwarranted, unmerited, and unexpected (Titus 3:4–8)—stemming from God's very essence, that is, his self-surrender. In a sense, there could be no other way if God is to be God.

However, as mentioned in the Theology of Exchange, the Spirit of self-surrender is also part of human identity. This being the case, it stands to reason that the Spirit of self-surrender, the Trinitarian Spirit *ad intra,* and the Spirit of Jesus, which is the same Trinitarian Spirit *ad extra* (completely accepted/received within created reality, namely Jesus of Nazareth), will echo quite naturally within human existence that which is actualized in its perfect Expression, Jesus of Nazareth. The note which is echoed is Sonship. Jesus, in accepting/receiving the Spirit, accepted as his identity his Sonship.

Throughout his life, Jesus lives out his reality as Son, that is, an attitude of abiding, selfless abandon to the Father. This is witnessed in the Gospel narratives which mark Jesus' life with sundry examples of surrendering. There we see that the heart of

Jesus' personal identity, the very core of his "I", is found in God, in the Father's address to him and in his response to the Father.[19]

As his own awareness and acceptance deepened, so too his living out the mission of the Spirit deepened. Finally, being obedient unto death, Jesus embraced his Sonship totally and completely; his humanity could not "contain" the accepting/receiving any longer. Totally and completely Son of God and son of Mary, he offered his entire Person to the Father (self-surrender) so the Father, in receiving all back from the Son, could create for him a new body (St. Paul calls it a spiritual body) within which the eternal exchange of self-surrender could be continued. All this occurs "in the Spirit," which is why the Spirit must be poured out anew on all.

Please note that the key element here is Jesus' Sonship accepted and received in the Spirit. Though Jesus always "had" the Spirit from the very beginning of his human life (the sanctificatory Spirit), he received and accepted (there is necessarily a process involved here if Jesus' humanity is to be preserved) the Spirit of Sonship at the River Jordan (the consecratory Spirit).[20] This was his Pentecost event; this was his mission statement: that he was self-surrender in his core, and, therefore, would surrender self in obedience to the Gift given him by the Father—the Gift of the Spirit of Sonship, the Gift of the eternal exchange of Trinitarian Love *ad intra,* which was his as the Eternal Son.

Since the same Spirit is in the Trinity, in Jesus of Nazareth, and in men and women, one might say that the basic, human experience is to live temporally that self-surrender which is eternal in God, witnessed in the person of Jesus of Nazareth, possible for us now through our union with Christ in the power of his Spirit. In short, it is nothing other than the imitation and reflection of that God who surrendered his very own Son for us,[21] living the self-surrender of the God who made us in his image and likeness.

MADE IN GOD'S IMAGE AND LIKENESS

We turn now to scripture and the tradition of the Church in order to deepen our understanding of humanity's need for reconciliation, as well as to probe its origin within human existence. Please note that sundry cultures and religions have formulated varied expressions regarding this subject, as it applies to their lived experience. Within the Christian context, however, it is believed that the history of salvation, as presented in the Old Testament and culminating in Jesus of Nazareth's life, death, and resurrection, is the fullest expression of God's operating in our midst. Rather than argue the validity or non-validity of other faith expressions regarding this, our presentation will be limited to the basic

Christian expression with references and images that are part of the Christian tradition.

In his book, *The Experience Called Spirit,* John Shea notes a basic human reality: we all desire to be loved.[22] This deep-rooted thrust within the human being stretches us toward sundry experiences, all of which fall short in realizing this internal desire. Nevertheless, a person often thinks that the goal has been reached, thereby leading him/her to grasp and cling to the object, the concept, or the person which seems to satisfy his/her quest. Time, however, always wins, leaving the individual with a tarnished treasure, regardless of how fulfilling it may have appeared at any given moment.

The reason for such failure does not stem from the person alone, but from the nature of the desire: a heart's infinite yearning can only be satisfied by an infinite Love, for the reality of God's presence (his image and likeness) hidden within our human limitations and finitude, stirs a yearning and a longing for the complete realization and actualization of our desire to be loved by Love. This Love, both as offer and response, is the mystery of self-surrender exemplified by Jesus in the totality of his self-surrender to the Father and the fullness of the Father's self-surrender to him.

In recalling to mind the Theology of Exchange paradigm, therefore, one can identify this longing as the fact of God's incomprehensible presence, his uncalled-for self-surrender within the individual. It is the fact of the Spirit breathed into us (cf.

Gn 2:7b) so that life might emerge; the fact of God's very own image and likeness unfolding within, reaching out, stretching toward the eternal embrace of Love which is the Trinitarian God's grounding and surrounding all.

This yearning and stretching is not something which may or may not happen. Rather, it is the very condition of all life which is human, even in the most humdrum of settings, for men and women are always and already on the way to God whether it is known expressly or willed intentionally.[23]

A Scriptural Picture

The origin of this yearning and craving is pictured in Genesis, which offers two stories of creation. In Genesis 1:27:

God created man in the image of himself,
in the image of God he created him,
male and female he created them.

and in Genesis 2:7b: "[Yahweh God] blew the breath of life into his [humankind's] nostrils, and man [and woman] became a living being."

We were made to walk in the garden with our Maker, to converse with him, to commune with him (cf. Gn 3:8). The "breath" that he gave us was his very life, his creative Spirit. It was this breath which granted us, in historical time, an identity springing from God's very being; it was this Spirit which, when given in historical time, enabled us to possess the image and likeness of God. We could now "be" like God. His Trinitarian identity, in a sense, was surrendered to us.[24] It would now be our identity. He shared himself with us in such a way that the binding power of his Love, the Spirit, the self-surrender which was and is his Being, was now to be the Source of our identity in time. It is not perchance that the psalms continuously refer to us as "sons [and daughters] of God," or that Paul reminds us it is the Spirit within who enables us to cry, "Abba."

In an analogous way, one might say that our human identity is "identified" by God similar to the way that the Eternal Word is "identified" by God as Son, to whom the Father offers everything; similar to the way the Eternal Word, the Son, "identifies" the Father by receiving from him—who is Source—all as Gift, and returning all as Gift, not clinging or possessing anything as his own; similar to the way the Spirit is the "identifying" reality which allows the Father to know the Son, and the Son to know the Father as Love offered and received and exchanged.

The fact we are made in God's image and likeness makes us children of God. This reality is based on the love which God offers us first. In Sermon 34, Augustine expresses this scriptural tradition quite clearly:

There is not one who does not love something, but the question is, what to love. The psalms do not tell us not to love, but to choose the object of our love. But how can we choose unless we are first chosen? We cannot love unless someone has loved us first. Listen to the apostle John: "We love him, because he first loved us." The source of man's love for God can only be found in the fact that God loved him first. He has given us himself as the object of our love, and he has also given us its source. What this source is you may learn more clearly from the apostle Paul who tells us: "The love of God has been poured into our hearts." This love is not something we generate ourselves: it comes to us "through the Holy Spirit who has been given to us."

Since we have such an assurance, then, let us love God with the love he has given us. John tells us more fully: "God is love, and whoever dwells in love dwells in God, and God in him."[25]

The Exchange Is Broken

It's hard to imagine God as eternally being Father, Son, and Spirit. We normally think in terms of sequence and time, whereas the eternal exchange that is the Triune God has no beginning. It was not as if the Father acted first, then the Son, then the Spirit. All was in action always.

It should also be pointed out that the eternal exchange of self-surrender, God's Reality, appears to involve a type of risk-taking. Difficult though it is to imagine, even in God there is no "guarantee" that the Gift offered by the Father would be received or exchanged by the Son. To remove the risk is to remove the freedom involved in divine self-surrender, Divine Love. Since this risk exists within God, it stands to reason that it also existed in God's act of creation, especially in his creation of men and women. As with the Father, Son, and Spirit, there was no guarantee that men and women, made in God's image and likeness, would indeed receive the gift offered, and exchange the gift received by sharing it with others. It is here that sin appears.

Genesis offers us several descriptions of sin entering the world: Genesis 3 (the serpent), Genesis 4 (Cain and Abel), Genesis 6:5f (the flood), and Genesis 11 (Tower of Babel). Since the serpent story is the most familiar, we will focus our attention there. By using the story, I do not mean to advocate or claim its "historicity," but to indicate the reality of sin, and reflect upon that reality.

We know the story well: the serpent tempted Eve to eat the fruit from the forbidden tree; she, in turn, convinced Adam to do the same. In light of the Theology of Exchange paradigm presented, the story might be viewed in the following light.

Believing the Lie

Eve was convinced by the serpent to believe the lie, namely, that God had not surrendered his complete self in creation; that God had held back, that is, fallen short in his offer of love. It was apparent, the serpent teased, that by eating of the fruit from the forbidden tree, your "eyes will be opened and you will be like gods, knowing good from evil" (Gn 3:5).

The truth of the matter was radically different. Adam and Eve were already like God since they were made in his image and likeness. This is borne out in the Hebrew notion of the word "image," which "relates to the root idea of something that is like another in the way that a man's [or woman's] shadow is like him, as in the bright sunlight, it falls on the ground, a clear and concrete shape."[26]

The forbidden fruit had nothing to do with being like God, but dealt with fidelity and obedience, listening to the voice of love. Could Adam and Eve be satisfied with all the Father offered rather than try to acquire as their own that which was not from him, that which was not the Source of their identity? Sin entered the world, therefore, because Adam and Eve failed to receive/accept what God had offered (his image and likeness). Instead, they sought a false source of identity (the forbidden fruit).

The repercussions were legion. By accepting the

lie, Adam and Eve began to live the lie, that is, to
treat one another as less than children of God, less
than brother and sister one to the other. Rather
than calling each other forth into his/her own
proper identity in relationship to God and to one
another, they began to hide, to blame one another
—"It was the woman you put with me; she gave me
some fruit from the tree, and I ate it" (Gn 3:12)—to
see each other's nakedness, to fail in accepting responsibility for actions taken—"The snake tempted
me and I ate" (Gn 3:13).

In short, separated now from the Source of their
identity, they experienced a sense of alienation,
driving them to find their identity through other
means, using their own wiles. They became individualistic, self-seeking, grasping false notions of life,
thereby bringing about death of body and spirit.
One now had to be over the other, one now had to
be subjugated so the other might look higher.[27] This
should not surprise us, according to John 8:44,
since Satan is the father of lies:

> He [Satan] was a murderer from the start;
> he was never grounded in the truth;
> there is no truth in him at all.
> When he lies
> he is speaking true to his nature,
> because he is a liar, and the father of lies.

The original plan was union; the original sin was
lack of trust which broke the exchange of love and

life given by the Source of all: the Father through the Son in the Spirit. This break caused the deep-rooted alienation which is characteristic of our life. Separated by choice from the only true Source of life, men and women became disoriented and root-less: aliens in the world they were suppose to in-herit. This alienation is, of course, the biblical cate-gory for sin.[28]

God's Plan Continues to Unfold

The scriptures continuously emphasize that all are caught in this reality, the bondage of the lie. Paul, for example, states: "We have already in-dicted Jews and Greeks as being all alike under the dominion of sin" (Rm 3:9); "No distinction is made: all have sinned and lack God's glory" (Rm 3:23); "Well then; it was through one man that sin came into the world, and through sin death, and thus death has spread through the whole human race because everyone has sinned" (Rm 5:12). John echoes this theme by reminding us, "If we say, 'We have no sin,' we are deceiving ourselves, and truth has no place in us" (1 Jn 1:8).

All, however, was not lost. After each account of the Fall, the authors of Genesis countered the de-struction of sin's entrance with God's reaching out and assisting the sinner: God helps Adam and Eve by clothing them; he protects Cain with a special sign place on his forehead; he saves Noah from the flood; and, after the final story of the Fall, the

Tower of Babel, God reveals his plan of covenant love to Abraham. The tradition of God's continued love held by the Chosen People is remembered in Deuteronomy 30:19: "Today, I call heaven and earth to witness against you: I am offering you life or death, blessing or curse. Choose life . . . ."

It must be emphasized at this point that the reality of sin expressed throughout the scriptures is pictured principally as a condition, not an action. This, in turn, has led the church to teach

> . . . that we begin our lives wounded, with a wound that touches the very core of our being. It is this wound that sets us warring within our own selves, one part against the other. It is this same wound, when actualized in our decisions, that leads to our own wrong actions. It is what theologians refer to as original sin.[29]

The difference between these two points of view is extremely important for a proper understanding of reconciliation. If we see sin principally as an action, we could easily equate sin with something dirty, usually of a sexual nature; or forgiving of sin with financial indebtedness; or committing sin with people doing things they should not be doing. Theological tradition, however, speaks of sin in the singular: not so much our bad actions, but our condition, which is likened to an illness, common to all. A condition which is a wound in our nature—a wound that leads us to strive destructively within ourselves and, in the outer world, against one another. Aquinas, asking whether God came into the world for the forgiveness of our sins in the plural or sin in the singular—original sin—opts for the forgiveness of original sin.[30]

God continues to be true to himself, continues to hold fast to the original plan of self-surrender by encouraging us to choose life. This life, of course, eventually took flesh in the Eternal Word incarnate, Jesus of Nazareth. Knowing this, St. Paul reminds us that God's very kindness and love is what leads us to repent and choose life again—to choose the Source of our life and our identity (Rm 2:4).

And so the plan unfolds. He who knew no sin (2 Co 5:21), that is, he, the Eternal Word who was always part of the Trinitarian exchange, became sin and, though never distant from God, chose to become a slave (Ph 2:6–8) by receiving flesh from the womb of Mary. This was done in order to fulfill and complete the original plan, so that one made in God's image and likeness would receive and accept his identity offered through the self-surrender of God to his creature. In Jesus, therefore, our true identity as God's children is revealed again, as in the awakening of a long-lost memory of the true self: we are created to accept the self-surrender of the Father and return it in the Spirit by living a life of self-surrender through the love we bear one another.

This is actualized in Jesus' very life, death, and

resurrection: the Suffering Servant stance he chose to accept; the Beatitudes he chose to live; his care and concern for the poor, the prisoner, the sick, the sinner. It all comes to fruition and fulfillment, completion and realization in his dying on the cross (1 P 3:18). Here he accepted even death as the sign of the Father's Gift of self-surrender to him, willingly embracing it, and returning it to the Father in trust: ". . . into your hands I commit my spirit" (Lk 23:46). Here Jesus completed the exchange when he trusted that God did not hold back, did not fall short in his Gift of self-surrender. Here Jesus is obedient unto death, thereby negating the disobedience of Adam and Eve.

And so, the Spirit is once again operative as intended (scripturally this is seen as sending the Spirit) because the exchange is complete. The solidarity of God's creation to himself is realized in Jesus, and so is realized in all. St. Paul says it this way: "If we have died with him, then we shall live with him" (2 Tm 2:11). This is simply saying that through his acceptance of death, Jesus remained faithful to the human condition; he trusted and accepted the gift given by the Father—death being part of that gift. Adam and Eve, however, were not faithful to the Source of their identity. They did not trust that the gift given would enable them to live forever. This lack of trust led them to infidelity, and to rejection of the gift of human life which was filled with the Spirit. Ironically, this lack of trust brought about the very thing they tried to avoid, namely death. Those who unite themselves to Jesus, therefore, are empowered through the Spirit to follow the way of fidelity and obedience.

Jesus reconciles us to the Father. Going back to our pictorial definition in the Introduction, he makes us "even" with the Father, although we originally failed to trust in his plan. He does this "for no reason except his own faithful love" (Tt 3:5), uniting us to God, yet maintaining the distinction between creature and Creator.

SOCIAL DIMENSIONS OF SIN

Because the Spirit—eternally present as the binding Love of Father and Son, historically given to Jesus, and raising him from the dead—is the same Spirit given to all, we can expect the Spirit to move within us in the same way that the Spirit moves within the Trinity, and within Jesus. This is the direction of self-surrender: giving one's self in love and service to others. There is no other way if we are to be faithful to the Spirit given us, faithful to ourselves, and faithful to God's image and likeness identifying us in the very creation of our humanity. St. Paul emphasizes this by calling us "ambassadors for Christ" (2 Co 5:20). It is our responsibility, in being true to our identity as children of God, to proclaim in word and deed the Good News that all are reconciled, that is, created as children of God:

> I mean, God was in Christ reconciling the
> world to himself, not holding anyone's faults
> against them, but entrusting to us the message
> of reconciliation . . . it is as though God
> were urging you through us, and in the name
> of Christ we appeal to you to be reconciled to
> God. (2 Co 5:19-20)

Reconciliation cannot stop with an individual's relationship to God. Having heeded the inner voice which calls him/her to conversion, the individual must proceed toward a change of heart which affects not only his/her own self-identity as child of God, but also his/her own response to others as children of God. Our society, clothed with a rugged individualism that mistrusts and denigrates sharing life's resources (and graces) with others, has a diminished capacity for appreciating the consequences of true reconciliation. Too often the process is left incomplete, thereby bending the effects out of shape.

If we accept the reality of reconciliation, the reality of our identity as children of a loving God, then we must necessarily share that reality with one another. This is the principal challenge facing Christians today: to integrate within our lives the notion of sin and the reconciling power of Jesus as a reality that is part and parcel of our human condition and possibility. It is not enough to assign to sin a problem-solving mentality. Problems can be solved whereas sin cannot be solved; it can only be forgiven and healed. Such talk, however, is somewhat out of fashion today. Perhaps we have seen so much that a direct look at the sin and evil in the world might threaten to overwhelm us.[31] Yet, to talk about reconciliation while ignoring our human capacity to sin, or to acquiesce before sin without proclaiming the reconciling power of Jesus, is to miss the point of our God-given freedom and his plan for us to freely choose him in the self-surrender of Christ.

Hopefully it is evident that more than personal sinfulness is involved here. There are also the more obvious injustices and violations that are part of our world—ones which we take for granted simply because they are so pervasive and subtle.[32] For example, sin rears its ugly head every time we fail to treat another as a child of God; every time we act or speak in ways that hinder another's discovering the truth of his/her identity, that he/she is a child of God; every time through word or deed we perpetuate the lie rather than reveal the truth. This is social sin at its core.

The possibilities of sin remain legion. Whenever structures are permitted, or fostered, or encouraged, or sought which take away the person's dignity as a child of God, loved and forgiven by the Father, we have failed as ambassadors of reconciliation and have acquiesced to sin; whenever people are permitted to manipulate, subjugate, or cheapen the life of another human being, we have failed to be reconcilers with Jesus, and have acquiesced to sin; whenever we profit from another's hardship or pain, we have failed to allow the Spirit of God within us to unfold according to God's original plan and have acquiesced to sin. David O'Rourke summarizes this predicament:

> In our eminently individualistic age it is easy to overlook the social role of religion, of Christian living, and of theology. Yet in the Catholic tradition this social role is a very important one, and today it serves as one of the principal countercultural and prophetic aspects of the Church's life.[33]

Perhaps the break came as theology compartmentalized and dissected the Christian's life in the Spirit into such precise truths that the truth of the parts overshadowed the integrated truth of the whole. Regardless, one must never forget that the gift given (reconciliation) must be shared in the same way that it was shared with us—regardless of cost. Dag Hammarskjöld's exhortation rings true: "The price you pay for your own liberation through another's sacrifice is that you in turn must be willing to liberate in the same way, irrespective of the consequences to yourself."[34]

The Social Dimension Broadens: Systemic Sin

The elements which led to a more complete understanding of social sin are varied: the biblical-patristic movement within contemporary theologi-

cal inquiry, Vatican II's reawakening of our understanding of the Church, the new consciousness of
co-responsibility existing within the Church community, as well as the contemporary, secular sense
of human solidarity and interdependence in poli-
tics, economics, and society at large.[35] No longer
can we remain isolated. We have become a true
global village in which each individual affects the
other. This shift in awareness leads to the following
insight: "Not only individual humans can be sinful;
social groups and whole societies can be corpo-
rately sinful."[36] In developing a theology of reconciliation, therefore, this reality must be addressed.

For those who have eyes to see and ears to hear,
the reality of systemic sin is no secret. Here also,
alienation, a basic concept of sin within the biblical
tradition, is easily applied: social and racial preju-
dices divide one group of people from another,
thereby intensifying the experience of alienation;
class struggles dominate human life where the poor
and the powerless fight for the freedom of human
dignity; women, conscious of the injustice that has
dominated them for centuries, fight to be recognized as equal to men; the rich and powerful fight
to increase their holding and control over those already subjugated. Such is the rotten fruit of systemic sin, rooted in the individual's and community's alienation from God, the true source of identity
and power.

Aided by the Spirit's gift of discernment, and the
expertise of men and women proficient in the social

and behaviorial sciences, systemic sin is being un-
covered for what it really is: believing the lie. Entire
nations, societies, and institutions have, in fact, embraced the very lie which itself roots all sin. Though
difficult to pinpoint any particular individuals for
committing such sin, decisions being made within
the business, industrial, and political order literally
exploit, manipulate, and enslave people with the lie
that they are less than God's son/daughter. By
maintaining environments which do not foster and
affirm sonship/daughtership, such systems institutionalize sinful activity by fostering attitudes, val-
ues, and structures which are not life-giving. They
institutionalize the lie, thereby giving it a newfound
power and opportunity to deceive.

Jesus Overcomes Social and Systemic Sin

To understand how Jesus' victory embraces the
total social dimension, it is important to view the
Church as the "community-Body of Christ and
the sacrament of salvation."[37] In this perspective,
the Church is seen as the gathering of those who
consciously stand against the lie of the world which
proclaims, through manipulation and exploitation,
that we are not beloved of God.

In this "community-Body of Christ," men and
women gather as one, striving to live as Jesus lives
by affirming the individuality of the person loved by
God as his very own. This is done in word and
action: with lives that attempt to proclaim and to

be God's Good News for all. Some call this the true work of evangelization, and intrinsic to Jesus' ministry of social reconciliation.[38]

Jesus embodies this reality. He who is the Eternal Word of God spoke the forgiving, healing words of love which men and women craved to hear. In his flesh he embodied these forgiving, healing words so that the love of the Father could be "seen with our own eyes, . . . watched and touched with our own hands" (1 Jn 1:1). To the extent that the "community-Body of Christ" is faithful to this embodied reality, it becomes the paradigm of all that human life can be. Here, within the living "community-Body of Christ," the eternal source of true identity (the Spirit) becomes the guiding and animating force of corporate life. No longer is one individual struggling alone to be and live his/her identity as son/daughter; no longer is one individual buffeted by society's desire to control and conquer, struggling alone to embody the beatitudes of Jesus; no longer is one individual forced to rely on his/her own receptivity to the transforming power of the Spirit. Now it is the entire "community-Body of Christ" as son/daughter that becomes the lived proclamation of God's reconciling presence in the world, the very embodiment of Jesus' beatitude lifestyle, the visible reservoir of the Spirit's transforming power in the world—a saving sacrament for all.

Jesus, therefore, brings about social reconciliation through the ministry of his chosen people, his

Body, who, united to him in the power of the Spirit, reveal the truth of God's original plan: we are made in his image and likeness; we are his sons and daughters, not tomorrow, but today.

3 / CELEBRATING THE SACRAMENT

Having the historical development of the sacrament as a reference, and a theological perspective as a guide, we can now look at the Sacrament of Reconciliation as celebrated by the Church in today's world. Our approach will be practical and descriptive. Starting with a general exposition of the sacrament as it applies to the three types of celebrations (rites) currently available, each of the three rites will be explained, highlighting the *Rite for Reconciliation of Individual Penitents,* since this is the one most commonly used in the Church. Emphasis has been placed here in order to assist the individual penitent in his/her celebration of the sacrament, since an understanding of this particular rite will enable an individual to celebrate the other rites with joy and faith. Pastoral reflections on the three rites will be offered in the next chapter, as well as some thoughts concerning the experience of God's forgiveness through channels other than the Sacrament of Reconciliation.

THE SACRAMENT OF RECONCILIATION AND ITS PARTS: AN OVERVIEW

Charged with implementing the Second Vatican Council's decree that "the rite and formulas of penance are to be revised in such a way that they may more clearly express the nature and effects of this sacrament,"[1] the Congregation for Divine Worship prepared a new *Rite of Penance* so the Catholic community might more fully experience and enjoy the fruit of Christ's victory over sin and death. We have already seen how this sacrament has been celebrated, in varying ways, throughout the centuries. It should not take us by surprise, therefore, that the Spirit's guiding power would also be evident in our own century.

Accordingly, in 1973, Pope Paul VI approved the new rite with its pointed emphasis on the relation of the sacrament to the community celebrating in the context of God's Word. Besides the expected *Rite for Reconciliation of Individual Penitents,* the Pope also approved a *Rite for Reconciliation of Several Penitents,* and, for special occasions, a *Rite for Reconciliation of Several Penitents with General Confession and Absolution.* Depending on the circumstances, the Church holds that each is a valid way of celebrating the sacrament.

Regardless of the rite used, the first and most important element of the Sacrament of Reconciliation is the presence and power of the Holy Spirit. It is here in the prompting of God himself, the Spirit of Love present to us, that we as sinners are "moved" beyond our sin. Were it not for this initiating grace of God we would remain forever chained, caught in the lie, aching with a pain that has no end. Yet the Spirit, moving upon God's people with love and mercy, coaxes us to return to the Source of Life and Love—even though individuals may not know it is the Spirit's calling and guiding.

It is the Holy Spirit, therefore, who leads us to the Sacrament of Reconciliation, breathing within us the desire to experience and know the Love that satisfies our needs, heals our wounds, and restores us to our original identity—children of a loving Father. Moved in this way, the believer necessarily approaches the Sacrament of Reconciliation with a heart ready for conversion, ready for change, ready to embrace sorrow for sin with the intent of leading a new life.

Through the leading of the Spirit, the believer responds to this prompting by inviting God to change his/her whole person. Realizing that words are not enough unless they spring from heartfelt contrition, the believer is expected to yield to the power of the Spirit so that the process of conversion, of *metanoia,* can take place. The efficacy of the sacrament is closely connected to this heartfelt contrition, for without it the movement of the Spirit is aborted. This has always been held by the Church: the grace of the sacrament is stymied unless we freely allow God to change us, and then begin to act accordingly. Contrition generated by the Spirit's prompting, is an important act on the part of the believer receiving the Sacrament of Reconciliation.

In addition, the sacrament includes the confession of sins, always made in the light of God's mercy. One is asked to "confess," not in an accusatory way, but as a way of acknowledging the very saving power and presence of God acting in our life. In acknowledging our sins, we also acknowledge that we are not God, and that only God is God. We acknowledge our need to be forgiven by the only one who can forgive—God himself. We present our limitations, our finiteness, our false self-identity to God so that he can grant us anew the embrace of love which defines and identifies us as his children.

Confession of sins is necessary regardless of which rite is being celebrated. When the *Rite for Reconciliation of Several Penitents with General Confession and Absolution* is celebrated, the one "who has had serious sin remitted by a general absolution is to approach individual confession as soon as there is an opportunity to do so before receiving another general absolution unless a just cause intervenes" (Canon 963).[2]

Having confessed our sins, we begin to engage in the remedy for sin, namely, penance. By performing certain actions which are suited for the particular offenses confessed, we are encouraged to reorganize and reprioritize our life so that the way of Jesus can be more manifest in everyday actions. Penance is more than paying a debt to God. Nothing we can do will ever balance out our offenses. Only Jesus' total acceptance of the Father's love was able to right the wrongs committed. Three Hail Marys and two Our Fathers, unless spurring us toward a change of direction, are far from an adequate penance. It is necessary, therefore, that "the act of penance really be a remedy for sin and a help to renewal of life."[3]

Finally, each of the rites includes absolution, the sign through which God's pardon is visibly ministered by the Church.

THE RITE FOR RECONCILIATION OF INDIVIDUAL PENITENTS

There are six parts to this particular rite:

Reception of the Penitent
Reading of the Word of God
Confession of Sins and Acceptance of Penance
Prayer of the Penitent
Absolution
Proclamation of Praise of God and Dismissal

Reception of the Penitent

This first step presupposes that a certain amount of preparation has taken place on the part of both penitent and priest. The preparation time is expressed at the very beginning of the celebration when the priest is called upon to greet the penitent warmly. A handshake, an embrace, a kiss, or a word of encouragement would be an appropriate sign. It should be noted that you (or the priest) may feel uncomfortable with these gestures. Try not to focus on your initial feeling, or the possible discomfort of the priest. Look, rather, at the message that the sign is trying to express: one of greeting, compassion, and love.

In line with this, as a priest who often ministers God's love in this sacrament, I find it necessary to prepare myself in prayer for the Spirit's using my entire human being as a channel of his grace. There are times when my body language may not communicate a welcoming attitude. Then I need to be aware of my limitations and ask the Spirit to help me overcome the barrier I might be presenting to the penitent. On the other hand, as a penitent you may find it helpful to ask the Spirit's assistance in overcoming any fears or discomfort you have in accepting an expression of God's love as it is communicated through another human being, namely the priest.

Having been welcomed warmly and greeted with

kindness, the penitent makes the sign of the cross, after which the priest invites him/her to trust in God. This "invitation" may be expressed in these or similar words (see *Rite of Penance,* 69–71, for additional prayer examples):

> May God, who has enlightened every heart,
> help you to know your sins
> and trust in his mercy.

to which the penitent answers,

> Amen.

Note that from the very beginning, the penitent is expected to place himself/herself under the sign of Jesus' cross. This is more than a rote ritual by which a Catholic begins every or any prayer. It is a faith expression on the part of the penitent, for through the sign of the cross he/she acknowledges the victory of Jesus over sin and death *and* affirms his/her belief that this victory is granted to all in the name of God himself revealed as Father, Son, and Spirit.

Reading of the Word of God (Optional)

Either the priest or the penitent may bring a scripture passage to the celebration of the sacrament. Although it is "optional," seek to utilize this possibility as often as you celebrate the sacrament.

Should the priest for some reason fail to offer a
passage for reflection, come prepared with one that
has touched your heart. Every time the Word of
God is proclaimed in the scriptures, the power of
the Spirit is released anew. Reading God's Word
opens our heart to a deeper experience of God's
love and mercy. Read the words slowly; allow them
to sink deeply within your being so that God's healing power can soothe you. Too often we underesti-
mate the power present in God's Word when proclaimed within our community. Yet it is here that
we are reminded of God's promise, assured of his
love, convinced of his faithfulness; it is here that we
are called to repentance and forgiveness.

At times, the priest might summarize or para-
phrase a scripture story which relates God's mercy
in action, for example, the "Prodigal Son" in Luke
15:11–32. This is acceptable. A selection of texts is
offered in chapter 5 of this book to help you search
the scriptures for a passage that touches your heart.
Additional references can be found in the *Rite of
Penance,* 72–83, 101–201. We need not be limited to
a particular list. Any scripture text appropriate to
the occasion is acceptable.

Confession of Sins and Acceptance of Penance

An important part of the sacramental process is
the confession of sins. Our society, built upon an
individualistic mentality, often fails to acknowledge
the relationship between an individual's personal

actions and the effect they may have on others. We find it difficult to acknowledge wrongdoing to another person. Telling our sins to a priest may be problematic for some. Nevertheless, the Church, when celebrating the Sacrament of Reconciliation, maintains that the confession of sins is an integral part of the reconciliation process. The reasons for this are sundry. First, bringing things to the light is a traditional, scriptural way of overcoming the Evil One. When things remain in the dark, hidden from view, they tend to wear us down, eating away at our inner harmony. By confessing our sins we are able to bring our sinfulness from the darkness of deceit and despair into the light of God's love and mercy. In addition, by confessing our sins to the priest we are able to look honestly at our spiritual growth and well-being. Simply saying, "I know I've sinned," may indeed help us to acknowledge our sinfulness but does not help us perceive the areas that need reorganization. By being specific we are more apt to focus our attention on what the Spirit is doing in our life to bring us into harmony with the Gospel of Jesus.

In the past there was a great deal of emphasis on telling the *exact* number of times one committed a sin, and the *exact* description of the offense. Today, though number and kind are still helpful in discerning the movement of the Spirit in our lives, it is recommended that the penitent look at trends within his/her life. Try to avoid the "laundry list" approach, that is, rattling off many different kinds of offenses and the number of times that they were committed. It seems that the Holy Spirit, while granting us forgiveness of all our sins when we confess them with a sincere heart, leads us to overcome certain focused areas at any one particular time.

Finally, confession of sins is important because it enables us to praise our God. One would not confess a sin unless one were assured of being forgiven. Confession allows us to place our trust in God's forgiveness, praising him, through our confession, for his mercy and love toward us who are sinners.

Throughout this time, the priest may assist the penitent by offering him/her counsel and encouragement. Should the penitent falter because of embarrassment or fear, the priest would try to set the penitent's heart at ease by reminding him/her of Jesus' victory over sin and death, and the renewal that is offered to all who enter into the paschal mystery. Sometimes a penitent runs out of words, or cannot articulate the feelings that are being experienced. During those times, the priest can be especially helpful through his patient listening, additional gestures of concern and love, such as a hand placed gently on the individual's shoulder, or simply by suggesting words and phrases which may help the individual pinpoint and express his/her feelings. Because the Sacrament of Reconciliation is a powerful release of God's mercy, an individual who has not received the sacrament in a long period of time may find himself/herself overwhelmed by the Spirit's presence. Such a consolation (often manifested with tears) is a gift meant to encourage the sinner as he/she moves from the darkness of sin to the light of the Father's love.

Once our sins are confessed, the priest, adapting his counsel to the penitent's circumstances, will offer a penance which the penitent is invited to accept. As I have already mentioned, the penance is not meant to pay God back for the wrongs committed. It is meant to assist us in reorganizing and reprioritizing our lifestyle so that the sin which has kept us from imaging Jesus will be avoided and overcome.

By accepting a penance, we are accepting the responsibility to be trained and disciplined in habits that move us away from sin. For this reason, the priest may ask the penitent what penance would be best in achieving this goal. Should this occur, do not choose something outlandish or severe, but one which will help counteract the sins that have been confessed. Confessing the sin of gluttony, for example, might involve a penance which encourages fasting, while the penance for pride might call for service to the downtrodden; the sin of greed might be overcome by a penance which disciplines us in the area of almsgiving, while the penance for anger might move us to offer speedier apologies and reparation toward the one hurt by our anger.

Prayer of the Penitent and Absolution

Having confessed his/her sin, and accepted the penance given by the priest, the penitent is encouraged to move toward a prayer of the heart, that is, a prayer which expresses his/her sorrow. For some, the traditional "Act of Contrition" may be the prayer chosen to express the sorrow felt. Others may choose a scripture verse such as Luke 15:18; 18:13:

> Father, I have sinned against you
> and I am not worthy to be called your son
> [daughter].
> Be merciful to me, a sinner.

Or, you might prefer to memorize one of the Church's prayers, using it as a guideline to express your sorrow:

> My God,
> I am sorry for my sins with all my heart.
> In choosing to do wrong
> and failing to do good,
> I have sinned against you
> whom I should love above all things.
> I firmly intend, with your help,
> to do penance,
> to sin no more,
> and to avoid whatever leads me to sin.

Our Savior Jesus Christ
suffered and died for us.
In his name, my God, have mercy.

Additional prayers of this type can be found in the
Rite of Penance, 85–92, or in chapter 6.

Regardless of which form you choose, remember
that the words are meant to be heartfelt, that is,
springing from the depth of our being. There is no
need to be bound by any formal prayers at this
point of the celebration. The Church urges us to use
our own words, based on the examples she herself
offers in the rite. Do not be afraid to experiment
with different expressions of sorrow. At one time in
our life, a particular prayer or gesture may be well
suited to express our feelings. At another time, a
different form of expression may be helpful. The
key, of course, is for the words that are spoken to
be an honest statement of our inner desire to express sorrow and embrace contrition. Actions, not
feelings, are meant to judge the efficacy of the
penitent's prayer of sorrow. All the prayers in the
world will hold little weight in the Kingdom if our
hearts are not willing to let the prayer be a reality
for us.

I would suggest that you stretch yourself by
praying the "Prayer of the Penitent" in a spontaneous fashion. Although our Catholic tradition is
more versed with set or form prayers, it is important for the believer to learn how to rely on his/her
own patterns of communication and expression

when speaking with the Lord. A spontaneous prayer allows the penitent to discover a new level and depth of relationship with our God, eternally present to us in the Spirit of Jesus. One might begin during the initial time of preparation. Here, in the privacy and silence of our heart, we can start to articulate our sorrow. When alone in our room, we can speak the prayer aloud—confident that the only one who hears us is the Lord, who is forever listening for the call of his people. Then, as our confidence builds, we might want to utilize the opportunity offered in the Sacrament of Reconciliation. There, within the privacy of the reconciliation room, we can express our sorrow, confident that our prayer will not be judged by the priest, but accepted by the Lord.

After this is done (or perhaps while it is being done, depending on the style that the priest employs) the priest will place or extend his hand over the penitent's head. Often, if the reconciliation room is conducive to this, the priest may stand and lay both hands on the head or shoulders of the penitent. In our Catholic tradition, the gesture of "the laying on of hands" indicates the love of the Father, the presence of the Spirit, the unity we have one with the other. It is a very beautiful, scriptural gesture—one that is used in many different situations: ministering to the sick, for example. Obviously, if a confessional screen is between the penitent and the priest, this gesture loses the thrust of its meaning. Even in such a situation, the priest is encouraged to

at least extend his right hand as he says the words
of absolution:

God, the Father of mercies,
through the death and resurrection of his Son
has reconciled the world to himself
and sent the Holy Spirit among us
for the forgiveness of sins;
through the ministry of the Church
may God give you pardon and peace,
and I absolve you from your sins
in the name of the Father, and of the Son, †
and of the Holy Spirit.

To which the penitent answers:

Amen.

Proclamation of Praise of God and Dismissal

After the absolution, the priest continues:

Give thanks to the Lord, for he is good.

The penitent answers:

His mercy endures for ever.

Then the priest dismisses the penitent who has been
reconciled, saying:

The Lord has freed you from your sins. Go
in peace.

The purpose of this brief exchange is worth noting. Having been reconciled through the mercy of the Father revealed in Jesus and communicated to us today in the Spirit of the risen Lord, the penitent is further encouraged to appropriate the action and event which has taken place. The priest reminds him/her of God's goodness—a goodness which warrants praise and thanks on the part of those who have received such love. The penitent's response is a proclamation and a statement of fact, namely, that God's mercy endures. This final dialogue may be expressed in other ways (see *Rite of Penance,* 93). The basic tenor is to remain the same: a further proclamation of God's goodness, especially in the goodness revealed to us by the forgiveness of our sins.

Having been freed from sin, the penitent is now ready to enter into the world, carrying the peace which only the Lord gives. As stated in paragraph 20 in the *Rite of Penance* itself: "The penitent continues his conversion and expresses it by a life renewed according to the Gospel and more and more steeped in the love of God, for 'love covers many a sin' (1 P 4:8)."

THE RITE FOR RECONCILIATION OF SEVERAL PENITENTS WITH INDIVIDUAL CONFESSION AND ABSOLUTION

The purpose of this second rite is to clarify and typify the relationship between the individual and the community. Our sin is never in a vacuum. As a member of the Body of Christ, we affect one another in our good deeds and our bad. Sin is always social to a certain degree, requiring a social experience of reparation. The *Rite for Reconciliation of Several Penitents* is an attempt to bring that connection to the fore.

The Community Assembles

Once the community has assembled, a psalm, an antiphon, or an appropriate song is sung. The purpose of the song is twofold: the fact that all are singing the same words and melody has the effect of uniting the hearts and minds of the faithful; the song is meant to ready the community's heart to hear God's Word and receive his mercy. The song must be carefully chosen. The text should communicate the scriptural themes of God's faithfulness, love, mercy, etc.; the melody should be singable. There is little use in having the organist or folk group play a song which no one can sing because it's too difficult, or simply too silly to sing.

United in spirit by the Spirit himself, the community is now greeted by the priest. Several examples of the style and type of greeting expected are given in the *Rite of Penance,* 49, 94–96. After the greeting he or another minister speaks briefly about the importance and purpose of the celebration and the order of the service. There is no need for a "Penitential Rite" at this point, since the entire rite is a celebration of reconciliation. Rather, after a brief explanation, one which allays fears and indicates the direction that the service will take, the priest offers a prayer in the name of those gathered. This prayer may be in his own words provided it follows the examples given in the *Rite of Penance,* 45, 50, 97–100. The celebration of the Word of God follows.

Celebration of the Word of God

As mentioned in a previous section, the reading of the Word of God is important in the celebration of the sacrament. Without God's Word we would not have within our grasp the promise of God given throughout the ages. The Word of God is meant to be treasured and honored. It encourages us to "seek mercy" because the "mercy of the Lord endures forever." Several readings can be used at this time. An appropriate psalm response (preferably sung) can be included between the readings. Silence is encouraged to allow the Word of God to speak to those gathered. You would be amazed at what the

Lord will say where we open our hearts in silence to the echo of the Word proclaimed.

Please note it is God's Word, that is, the scriptures, which is to be read at this time. Although there is no question that the Lord's Spirit can and does speak to us in a variety of ways, the celebration of the Sacrament of Reconciliation should rest on the Word which is part of our inspired tradition. This does not mean that the minister may not utilize other readings as he explains the inspired Word of God. Rather, it allows us to place God's Word in the preeminent position it deserves. Should there be only one reading, it is preferable that it be from the Gospels.

Having proclaimed God's Word and encouraged the faithful with a homily based on the texts read, the priest, deacon, or other minister now leads the penitents in an examination of conscience. An example of this is given in chapter 6. The purpose of such an examination is to review and renew our lives. It is not meant to oppress us with guilt, or frighten us with an image of an angry God. Its purpose is meant to arouse sorrow in the hearts of the faithful, encouraging them to seek the Lord's mercy. Brief statements or a kind of litany, taking into consideration the circumstances, age, background, etc., of those participating, may be used.

Rite of Reconciliation

Responding to the examination of conscience, the community joins together praying a general formula for confession: "I confess . . ." for example. Any common text expressing sorrow and contrition may be used. This is followed by a litany or a song, ending always with the Lord's Prayer. Examples of this format are found in the *Rite of Penance,* 54, 202–5. It should be noted that the saying of the general formula does not remove the need for individual confession but is offered as a sign of solidarity one with the other, each acknowledging the general state of sinfulness existing in his/her life.

Having completed this, the "penitents go to the priests designated for individual confession, and confess their sins. Each one receives and accepts a fitting act of satisfaction and is absolved. After hearing the confession and offering suitable counsel, the priest extends his hands over the penitent's head (or at least extends his right hand) and gives him [her] absolution. Everything else which is customary in individual confession is omitted" *(Rite of Penance,* 55).

Proclamation of Praise

The rite continues with these instructions:

When the individual confessions have been completed, the other priests stand near the one who is presiding over the celebration. The latter invites all present to offer thanks and encourages them to do good works which will proclaim the grace of repentance in the life of the entire community and each of its members. It is fitting for all to sing a psalm or hymn or to say a litany in acknowledgement of God's power and mercy, for example, the canticle of Mary (Luke 1:46–55), or Psalm 135:1–9, 13–14, 16, 25–26 *(Rite of Penance, 56).*

This, in turn, is followed by the concluding prayer of thanksgiving *(Rite of Penance, 57, 207–11)* offered by the priest. The entire rite is brought to an end with a blessing by the priest *(Rite of Penance 58, 212–14),* and the dismissal by the priest, deacon, or some other minister. Oftentimes, the community will sing another song of praise, or the music ministers will play a recessional, as the priest and ministers leave the sanctuary.

THE RITE FOR RECONCILIATION OF SEVERAL PENITENTS WITH GENERAL CONFESSION AND ABSOLUTION

Church Guidelines for Celebration of the Rite

Before describing this particular rite, it might be helpful to understand when and how the Church uses this rite in celebrating the Sacrament of Reconciliation. Despite common opinion, the promulgation of the rite does not eliminate the responsibility we have as sinners to participate in individual, auricular confession. The Church maintains that this remains "the ordinary ways [sic] for the faithful to be reconciled to God and the Church unless physical or moral impossibility excuses from such confession" *(Pastoral Norms Concerning the Administration of General Sacramental Absolution,* I). Two possible situations are mentioned in this latter regard: when one is in imminent danger of death, or "in view of large number of penitents there are not enough confessors at hand to hear properly the confessions of each within an appropriate time, with the result that the penitents through no fault of their own would be forced to be without sacramental grace of Holy Communion for a long time" *(Pastoral Norms,* III). Such a decision is reserved to the local Ordinary after he has conferred with other members of the episcopal conference *(Pastoral Norms,* V).

Even when the rite is used, certain dispositions are required on the part of the faithful *(Pastoral Norms,* VI). Each should repent of the sin he/she has committed; have the purpose of keeping from sin; intend to repair any scandal or loss caused by the sin; have the purpose of confessing in due time each serious sin that he/she is at present unable to confess. "In due time" has been taken to mean within one year (cf. footnote 2 above). In celebrating the sacrament in this way, the priest has the responsibility to remind the penitents of their responsibilites and to exhort them toward sincere repentance.

The Celebration

For the most part, the celebration follows the same format as the *Rite for Reconciliation of Several Penitents with Individual Confession and Absolution.* After the homily, or as part of the homily, the priest explains to the faithful the dispositions necessary to receive the sacrament properly. Some sort of penance is imposed, and the individual is exhorted to add to the proposed penance a particular penance which is suited to his/her own circumstance. Then the priest, deacon, or other minister invites those who wish to receive absolution to indicate this by some sort of sign. Here a great deal of creativity is possible. The sign that is offered in the rite itself involves kneeling, or bowing one's head. Others can be used. Some find it helpful to arrange for the community to come forward and bless themselves with holy water as a sign of renewing their baptismal adoption as children of God; others find the presentation or offering of some personal gesture, for example, a prayer written during the silent time after the examination of conscience, to be effective. The most effective guideline is simplicity. It is recommended that one avoid complicated gestures or symbols that require lengthy explanations. If the sign or symbol chosen does not "speak for itself," that is, convey its meaning by its very use, then using such a sign should be reexamined.

Following such a gesture, the penitents say a general formula for confession, for example, "I confess . . ." A litany or appropriate song may also be included, always concluding with the Lord's Prayer.

Extending his hands over the penitents, the priest then offers absolution:

PRIEST: God the Father does not wish the sinner to die
          but to turn back to him and live.
          He loved us first and sent his Son into the world to be its Savior.
          May he show you his merciful love and give you peace.

RESPONSE: Amen.

PRIEST: Our Lord Jesus Christ was given up to death for our sins,
          and rose again for our justification.

He sent the Holy Spirit on his apostles
and gave them power to forgive sins.
Through the ministry entrusted to me
may he deliver you from evil
and fill you with his Holy Spirit.

RESPONSE: Amen.

PRIEST: The Spirit, the Comforter, was given to
us for the forgiveness of sins.
In him we approach the Father.
May he cleanse your hearts and clothe
you in his glory,
so that you may proclaim the mighty
acts of God
who has called you out of darkness into
the splendor of his light.

RESPONSE: Amen.

PRIEST: And I absolve you from your sins
in the name of the Father, and of the
Son, †
and of the Holy Spirit.

RESPONSE: Amen.

The priest may choose to use the shorter form of absolution noted in the two rites which were previously examined. Regardless of which option is chosen, the result is the same: forgiveness in the name of the Lord God is offered and received by the penitent. The rite draws to an end with a proclamation of praise, sometimes accompanied by a song or hymn, followed by the priest's blessing and dismissing the people.

4 / Pastoral Reflections

As noted in the historical treatment of the Catholic, Christian community's celebrating the Sacrament of Reconciliation, our one faith—remaining intact throughout the ages—utilized various procedures and rituals to communicate God's mercy to his people (cf. "Decree of Promulgation of the *Rite of Penance"*). In line with this attitude, the present *Rite of Penance* is correctly viewed as an instrument of God's mercy for the contemporary Church. Using that instrument, the Church instructs her people, and empowers her ministers to serve as reconcilers ministering the love and mercy of the Father revealed by Jesus Christ.

It would be incorrect, however, to view the present document as a fixed citadel, an immutable boundary within which God's mercy, henceforth and for all time, is meant to be experienced per se. We do not want the *Rite of Penance* to become an idol, thereby replacing the God who empowers us with his love. The Sacrament of Reconciliation, as celebrated by the Church in today's world, is better seen as an ongoing movement of the Spirit working within the Church's structures. As this ongoing movement enlightens and transforms us, we grow in openness to the discovery and celebration of the full truth of love revealed in Jesus, present to us in an enduring way through the power of the Spirit.

The document which encourages us to celebrate God's mercy in the Sacrament of Reconciliation, is a living act of the Church, one which reaches back through almost two thousand years of experience and tradition, and stretches forward toward an unlimited and undefined future.[1] It is important that one does not weight incorrectly the absoluteness of the rites promulgated, nor dismiss as relative the rites as they are celebrated within today's Church. We need not formulate norms and structures with any more absoluteness than the Church requires of her people. From the very beginning it is fruitful to acknowledge that our own historical limitations prevent us from perceiving all possible and permissible changes that will help us celebrate the full truth and abundance of the Father's forgiveness revealed in Jesus, and unfolding still through the power and presence of the Spirit.

WHAT DOES THE "RITE OF PENANCE" SAY TO TODAY'S CHURCH?

As a profession of faith in the mystery of reconciliation throughout our salvation history, the "Introduction to the *Rite of Penance*" offers us a general overview of God's love and mercy operative throughout history. Focused on the saving event of Christ's death and resurrection, the faithful are encouraged and exhorted to believe wholly in the love of the Father revealed to humanity through Jesus Christ. We are further encouraged to accept the reconciliation ministry of Jesus by utilizing with faith that ministry now carried on in the Church through the power of the Spirit.

Furthermore, the *Rite of Penance* reminds all members of the Church that they as a body are called to be a sign of humanity's conversion to God. This will be most powerfully realized as she (the Church) who is called to be the sign also remembers and acknowledges herself as the sinner in need of conversion and reconciliation. The Church is paradoxically proclaimed as both the instrument of reconciliation and the one in need of reconciliation. Though various ways of experiencing this reality are acknowledged, the Sacrament of Reconciliation is seen as the preeminent way that pardon from God and reconciliation to the Church is received.

It is unfortunate that the *Rite of Penance* does not break much new ground regarding any development of doctrine that has taken place in various theological disciplines which might affect the administration of the sacrament. Recalling to mind the historical survey in chapter 1, it can be noted that the administration of the sacrament was very much influenced by the historically based understanding of sin which was operative at the time.[2] The document's silence in this regard might be considered a deficiency, since it directs us toward a goal without offering guidelines necessary to understand why the journey is being taken in the first place.

It must be remembered that the document emerged during the time following Vatican II, a time best described as turbulent in both the secular and religious spheres. That the committee working on the document should choose not to address this question is quite understandable. However, recent developments in theology necessitate reflective examination in order to maintain a proper perspective and balance regarding the celebration of the sacrament.

Reconciliation or Penance?

The lack of theological clarity allows the document to accept an indiscriminate use of the word reconciliation. Although claiming that there is a distinction between reconciling those who have sinned gravely, and celebrating a devotional reception of the sacrament, the distinction seems to get lost as the document unfolds. In fact, the issue is confused by using the terms penance and reconciliation almost interchangeably. For example, the term reconciliation is applied to those who "have left the house of the Father" as well as those who have remained there, these being but two of almost a dozen different meanings offered with little logic or consistency.[3]

One may recall that the early Church used the term reconciliation to describe "overcoming the radical break with the community of believers, and with God, that takes place through a falling away from baptismal grace." In such a case public rites were needed (at least until the Middle Ages) which ritualized the individual's separation from the community, his/her intense ascetical reparation, and the liturgical act of reconciliation by the bishop.[4]

Penance, on the other hand, appears in the early Church to be a less dramatic process than reconciliation. Rather than restoring a break between the individual and the community, it was viewed as a comprehensive range of ascetical and sanctifying activities to which every faithful Christian was obliged. It was, in the words of John Paul II's *Apostolic Exhortation,* "the concrete, daily effort of a person, supported by God's grace, to lose his or her own life for Christ as the only means of gaining it." Penance was the ongoing conversion which was applicable to all, never absent from the life of a believer nor from the Church's ministry or liturgical self-expression.[5]

One can easily see how this might lead to a confusing pastoral procedure. If the *Rite for Reconciliation of Individual Penitents* is expected to accomplish two different objectives, namely, reconciliation after grave sin *and* the objective, ongoing, penitential transformation of the individual realized in confessions of devotion (cf. *Rite of Penance,* 7), it should not take us by surprise that an individual is no longer sure when and if he/she should receive the sacrament.

The document encourages frequent confession for the faithful, yet does not suggest how this might be effectively integrated into the life of the individual and the life of the Church. If we assume that the *Rite for Reconciliation of Individual Penitents* should be celebrated frequently, we must also devise a way that the dialogue encouraged between penitent and priest, and the spiritual discernment called for by the rite, is not diminished by overuse or the pressured time schedules present during holy days such as Christmas and Easter. The *Rite for Reconciliation of Several Penitents* could realistically alleviate this difficulty by helping the community experience and celebrate reconciliation for sins that are not grievous. This rite, however, remains limited by its insistence on individual confession and absolution.

The Rite for Reconciliation of Several Penitents

Closely connected to this is the question of communal penance services where individual confession and absolution take place. As demanded by the ritual, whenever the community gathers for the celebration of the Sacrament of Reconciliation, individual confession and absolution is necessary. This, unfortunately, creates logistically difficult pastoral situations which require further evaluation and re-

flection. Such a demand places an unreasonable
burden upon the staying power of the community.
It may take hours for a group of priests to hear the
confessions of hundreds of penitents. With the
shortage of clergy becoming more the norm than
the exception, a community can no longer assume
that an adequate number of priests will be available
to hear the confessions of a large number of individuals who are celebrating a communal penance service. This is not to eliminate or lessen the need that
the priest has to be available for lengthy periods of
time to minister to individuals within the Sacrament of Reconciliation.

Furthermore, within the context of a group's
gathering, there is a need to maintain a prayerful
spirit while the penitents are receiving individual
ministry. More often than not the length of the service diminishes the possibility of maintaining such
an atmosphere. If the penitents are dismissed, or
leave, before confessions are heard, the liturgical
flow of the rite is destroyed. However, by permit-
ting the community to confess generic sins existing
within the individual members as well as the membership united as one, the flow of the rite could be
maintained.

In addition, the *Rite for Reconciliation of Individual Penitents* emphasizes the dialogue and personal
attention that the individual is meant to receive
within the celebration of the sacrament. By insist-
ing that every penitent within the *Rite for Reconciliation of Several Penitents* must confess and receive

absolution individually, however, the dialogue and personal attention highlighted in the first rite must be submerged in the second rite, lest the celebration become too lengthy. Furthermore, the large number of penitents and the small number of priests almost guarantees the development of an "in and out" mentality, harking back to the days preceding Vatican II.

During that time, if one did not have any grievous sins to confess, the individual was encouraged to confess "small sins" or previously forgiven sins so that the proper matter for confession would be present. Upon inspection, such an approach left much to be desired. Confessing sins that were previously forgiven could not possibly constitute matter for confession, since the events confessed no longer existed as sins in the person's life. Nevertheless, the minister would dutifully give absolution in such situations, despite the lack of sin.

This being the case, it does not appear unreasonable to assume that a penance service in which individuals are not confessing a "sin unto death" might be an acceptable and desirable place for the community to receive absolution without confessing specific sins to the priest. Rather, individuals would confess generic sin through a litany or communal examination of conscience in conjunction with the community's communal confession. In doing so, the intensity called for in the first rite could be maintained, and the community could be led to experience more completely the variety of ways that the Lord offers forgiveness to individuals within the context of the community. This hinges, of course, on the following presupposition:

> If a fundamental break with God is an ordinary event in the Christian community, the ordinary practice should indeed be person to person reconciliation. If, on the other hand, such a break is as rare as the penitential discipline of the ancient Church presumed it, the ordinary practice may well be in communal repentance and common absolution.[6]

General Absolution

Another area requiring additional theological and pastoral clarity is the practice of general absolution. As noted in chapter 3 of this book, the *Rite of Penance* approved of the practice if certain circumstances were present. Recent statements by the Vatican, however, seem to muddy the water by appearing to curtail the Ordinary's right to decide when the necessary conditions exist. This discussion revolves around paragraphs 31 and 32 in the *Rite of Penance* (cf. Canon 961) which give the local Ordinary, in conjunction with episcopal conferences, the right to determine when general absolution may be necessary for the good of the people under his care. This, of course, is pastorally sound, since the local bishop would have a much better sense of the concrete, pastoral situation and the needs of the people.

The question that is raised is whether or not the "grave need" mentioned is to be applied univocally to the one example given, namely, "when, in view of the number of penitents, sufficient confessors are not available to hear individual confessions properly within a suitable period of time, so that the penitents would, through no fault of their own, have to go without sacramental grace or holy communion for a long time" or analogously to sundry applications dependent upon the needs of the people and the pastoral sense of the Ordinary. This, of course, has only caused confusion among the people: some dioceses continuing to interpret the guidelines within a broad context; others feeling obliged to follow the letter of the law.[7]

Fueling the controversy further is Canon 962 in the recent Code of Canon Law where a subtle change emerges. There, the validity of general absolution appears to rest upon the penitent's intention to confess all mortal sins. Previously, validity was not being questioned, although the penitent was morally bound to confess all grave sins at a later date. This raises an important question: If absolution is given, why would a person need to bring those sins into another sacramental act?[8]

Besides, what constitutes "intention"? Are we opening a Pandora's Box? As Orsy wisely states:

> In general, to legislate externally about internal acts, and to make the validity of a sacrament dependent on a thought or movement

hidden in the mind and the heart of a person, is always a delicate operation. One has just to think of the difficulties we are having all the time concerning the intention of the parties in concluding the marriage covenant. To introduce similar problems into the administration of the sacrament of penance can be justified only by some kind of divine law from which the Church cannot dispense. Otherwise an unnecessary burden is imposed, precisely at a moment when God is there to lift the burden of sins.[9]

An additional question centers around Canon 960 which states that the "individual and integral confession and absolution constitute the only ordinary way by which the faithful person who is aware of serious sin is reconciled with God and with the Church." No mention is made regarding those who are not conscious of serious sin. Would it be possible that in such a situation, the ordinary means might very well be general absolution?

Unspoken, but possibly underlying this controversy, is the fear that general absolution might eliminate or lessen the community's participation in the other two rites, especially in the *Rite for Reconciliation of Individual Penitents*. It appears to many that such a fear is unwarranted. My own (albeit limited) experience with the third rite confirms the observation of those who see general absolution as an important means of drawing individuals back to the experience of individual, auricular confession. Many Christians are fearful of receiving the sacrament using the form for individual confession. This cannot be ignored, even if these fears, often based upon misinformation or bad experiences of celebrating the sacrament due to an undiscerning minister, cannot be justified. The fact remains: people are less prone to celebrate the Sacrament of Reconciliation according to the rites of the Church. To deny this is to deny the pastoral reality surrounding us.

By allowing general absolution, especially during the Lenten season which emphasizes the call to repentance, the grace of God would be given an opportunity to further soften and transform the heart of the individual penitent. This would in no way lessen his/her need for individual confession. Quite the contrary. Having received God's forgiveness within an uplifting and affirming context, the individual might be more open to receive the sacrament within the context of individual confession. Note that the question here is not one of "cheap grace" or "the easy way out," but the celebration, on a sacramental level, of God's abounding love.

FUTURE DIRECTIONS FOR RECEIVING AND CELEBRATING FORGIVENESS

In the early Church, less serious sins were submitted to penitential discipline without the necessity of formal reconciliation. By doing so, a penitential lifestyle was able to develop within the Christian community. Fasting, almsgiving, vigils, pilgrimages, sharing in the suffering of Christ, carrying out works of mercy and charity were some of the ways that the people of God accomplished and perfected this continual repentance (cf. *Rite of Penance,* 4). This was the ordinary way that God's pardon was sought: by constantly nurturing a contrite heart and repentant spirit.[10] This can occur today in the liturgy "when the faithful confess that they are sinners and ask pardon of God and of their brothers and sisters" or "in penitential services, in the proclamation of the word of God, in prayer, and in the penitential aspects of the eucharistic celebration."[11]

In order to develop the penitential spirit among its members, the Church needs to exhort and teach the community that repentance—individual and communal—is, in fact, the ordinary way of life for the believer. This will necessarily involve priests who are trained and prepared to listen, who, striving to be healers of the individual and communal spirit, seek divine wisdom and help. It will necessarily involve people who are willing to struggle with the reality of good and evil in their lives, aware that sin does in fact separate us from the God who desires unity. It will require broadened horizons which do not absolutize the image of God, but remain open to Jesus, the never-ending beginning, who constantly breaks us and brings us out of our limited, absolute categories so that we can be remade in his image and likeness.

As this penitential spirit deepens within individuals, and within the community itself, the experience of communal penance services with sacramental absolution given in common might begin to bear fruit. In some ways, the development of this attitude is circular, that is, communal services and common absolution would help generate the penitential spirit and as the penitential spirit develops the communal penance services and common absolution would empower the community to embrace a penitential spirit. We might begin this process by focusing on communities that have a natural relationship to one another, where religious awareness is relatively high: for example, seminarians, religious orders, charismatic prayer groups, etc. In this way the experience can be monitored, and the fruit can be discerned.

It is in this area of communal penance services that we might place the experience of the child receiving First Eucharist. Fewer and fewer theologians and professional religious educators (not to mention parents, priests, and bishops) hold the opinion that a child can sin grievously at the age of six or seven. This is not to say that a child does not commit sin on a child's level. However, to think that a six-year-old can sever his/her relationship with God, thereby requiring the grace of the Sacrament of Reconciliation, simply goes against our experience. Developing a penitential spirit, however, and learning how to celebrate this, would be a natural way for a child to grow into a mature, sustaining faith. Proceeding in the direction that is presently being charted, that is, receiving the Sacrament of Reconciliation before First Eucharist, will only confuse the child, or fixate his/her faith development at the "magic" stage of belief.

It would not be proper to assign communal penance services in an exclusive manner to specially interested groups. Doing so would deny the general assembly the opportunity to grow in the faith. The celebration of reconciliation with general absolution, therefore, might also be offered to the Church during the penitential season of Lent. In this way, the grace of the sacrament could free the individual from the fear he/she might have of entering into the ordinary way of reconciliation of serious sin, namely, through individual confession and absolution. This is not playing games with the grace of the sacrament. Rather, it is placing one's trust in the power that is present in the sacramental celebration. The Spirit of the Lord, once accepted in any degree whatsoever, will naturally lead the person to the fullest experience and expression of unity with the Father. That, in fact, is the very "job" of the Spirit. Receiving valid absolution at a communal penance celebration might begin to prepare the individual penitent to move deeper into the experience of reconciliation. One must remember: the fact that sins are forgiven does not eliminate the need one has for a deeper lived experience of the reconciliation (unity) with the Father that forgiveness brings. Though completely forgiven, there is always "more" of the Father's love available.

Before concluding this section, the experience of healing must also be mentioned as a way of receiving and celebrating the forgiveness of the Father. The healing to which I refer might be called "inner healing," in that it touches the very core of our being. Work in this area is being done by Fathers Matthew and Dennis Linn, Michael Scanlan, Ms. Barbara Shlemon, et al.[12] Their experience points to the power implied in James 5:16–17 which exhorts the community to "confess your sins to one another, and pray for one another to be cured; the heartfelt prayer of someone upright works very powerfully."

One may, of course, object to confessing sins to another person. However, experience has shown that the "sins" to be confessed in this forum are more than likely "sins" which have been sacramentally forgiven. The situation is mentioned so that the residue or effect of sin can be alleviated. Traditionally the Church has always held that sin bears consequences which the person must learn to live with and to overcome. Though forgiven, the individual may still suffer the effects of the sin committed. Prayer for inner healing calls upon the power of the Lord to heal this inner wound so that the effect no longer has power over the individual. A simple example may help in understanding this experience. An individual who has been abandoned as a child, may, in fact, have forgiven the parent for the pain of separation that was suffered. However, the fact still remains: the individual experienced abandonment. This requires inner healing, lest the pain of abandonment continue to affect the person's human growth (this, of course, includes spiritual growth). For example, the pain of abandonment may become a barrier to the person's entering into any loving relationship since he/she is fearful of being abandoned again.

Many involved in the charismatic renewal are quite comfortable with this experience. Their energies and talents might be tapped for a more extended outreach to others within the parochial setting. Again, working with children in this way would be very beneficial for the Church's future. Children have fewer objections to praying with one another, or having an adult pray for them. In addition, they relish the group process that such a prayer experience offers. Beginning at an early age, urging children to seek forgiveness and healing from one another through healing prayer would prepare them to live more fully the Gospel of the

Lord. Examples of such prayer exercises may be found in chapter 7.

CONCLUSIONS

Despite drawbacks within the *Rite of Penance,* the basic document remains a pastorally positive step in the right direction. Lessons learned from the pastoral and liturgical renewal have had an impact and are now part of the Church's structured celebration. Each rite encourages creativity, calling for adaptation suitable for different groups and people. God's Word has been highlighted; priests are urged to be spontaneous in their prayer, and personal in their gestures. Reconciliation rooms are being designed which alleviate the penitent's fear of a darkened confessional. Healer rather than judge is becoming the predominant description of the Church's minister. All of this is pastorally sound. Theologically, however, additional reflection is necessary.

Education, of course, will be needed. Here we face the difficult task of educating not just our lay people, but our priests. Unfortunately, many do not use the new rite whatsoever, or use an abbreviated form. To think that the clergy has, in fact, accepted the new rite is to ignore the pastoral reality. Priests in the past have not been trained or encouraged to deal on a personal, discerning level with the penitent. The new rite demands that such an attitude be adopted. Priestly conversion will be needed—that which can only come through prayer and penance. The challenge is great, but the victory will be glorious, once the challenge is accepted.

Finally, legislators would be well advised to provide more provisional texts which might enable and empower various episcopal conferences throughout the world to apply the reconciliation ministry of Jesus to their particular situations. To assume that a centralized "clearing house" is able to devise one rite which answers everyone's needs, so many of which are culturally formed, is to limit the varied, human reality in God's creation. What needs "absolutizing" is the unimaginable reality of the Father's love. By "absolutizing" a particular ritual, however, we can easily lose sight of its purpose, namely, communicating the Father's mercy.

Of this it is certain: we are at an exciting time in the history of the Church. Together, as God's people reconciled in Jesus, we are called to move ahead toward the unlimited and unimagined mercy of the Father.

Postscript

We began with the story of a woman, and so, I would like to end with the story of a woman—a different-styled woman, to be sure, but a contemporary parable and example. Mother Angelica is the founder of the first Catholic satellite television network. A popular conference speaker, hosting many excellent Christian TV programs, she often shares personal experiences, one of which I would like to relate. I have adapted this incident from an article read in *New Covenant* magazine.

Mother Angelica was walking along an ocean beach. Clad in traditional garb, veil blown by the wind, she was skirting the edge of the waterline when suddenly, without warning, a huge wave broke and doused her with water. The poor sister was so surprised that she lost her balance and found herself sitting, rather unceremoniously, in the puddled sand. She felt quite ridiculous, and embarrassed. It was then, at that moment of weakness, that she sensed the Lord speaking to her in her heart.

"Angelica!" said the Lord.

Still trying to recoup her composure (the last one she wanted to hear from at the time was the Lord),

she was picking herself up when her eye caught
sight of a drop of water hanging from her finger.

She answered, "Yes, Lord."

"Angelica, do you see this bead of water?"

Not quite sure where this whole thing was leading, Angelica responded quite simply, "Yes, Lord, I
see it."

The Lord continued: "Angelica, if you were to
fling that drop into the sea, do you think you could
ever find it again?"

"No, Lord, I know I couldn't. The ocean is too
big."

"Angelica, that drop represents your sins—all
that you have committed. The sea is my unlimited
love for you: an ocean of mercy. You can either
hang on to the droplet of your sins and be miserable
with guilt, or you can fling it into the ocean of my
mercy where you will never be able to find it again.
Choose, Angelica. Which will you have?"

Without hesitating, she thrust the drop into the
sea.

And you? Which will you choose?

PART TWO

5 / BIBLICAL READINGS

The following scripture passages are proposed as a help for penitents, pastors, and others involved in the selection of readings. The list is by no means definitive. For diversity, and according to the needs of the individual or group, other readings may be selected in preparing to receive the sacrament, and/or in preparing a communal penitential service. The short phrase following a reading is meant to indicate the content of the reading; it is not meant to be used in place of the reading.

READINGS FROM THE OLD TESTAMENT

Genesis 3:1–19   The story of Adam and Eve and the Fall.

Genesis 4:1–15   The story of Cain and his brother Abel.

Genesis 18:17–33   The story of Sodom and Gomorrah. Yahweh would spare the city for the sake of ten good people.

Exodus 17:1–7   The Israelites put Yahweh to the

test, asking, "Is Yahweh with us, or not?" Moses strikes the rock and water flows.

Deuteronomy 6:3–9 "You must love Yahweh your God with all your heart, with all your soul, with all your strength."

Deuteronomy 9:7–19 Yahweh complains to Moses: "[Your people] have been quick to leave the way I marked out for them."

Deuteronomy 30:15–20 "Today I am offering you life and prosperity."

2 Samuel 12:1–9, 13 David said to Nathan, "I have sinned against Yahweh." Nathan then said to David, "Yahweh, for his part, forgives your sin; you are not to die."

Nehemiah 9:1–20 The Israelites, in sackcloth and with dust on their heads, assembled for a fast . . . [They] stood up and confessed their sins and the iniquities of their ancestors.

Wisdom 1:1–16 On seeking God and rejecting evil. Seek him in simplicity of heart.

Wisdom 5:1–16 The hope of the godless is like chaff carried on the wind . . . But the upright live for ever.

Ecclesiasticus 28:1–7 Pardon your neighbor any wrongs done to you.

Isaiah 1:2–6, 15–18 Your hands are covered in blood, wash, make yourselves clean.

Isaiah 5:1–7 The Song of the Vineyard: the Lord expected it to yield fine grapes, but they were wild ones.

Isaiah 43:22–28 I, I it is who blots out your acts

of revolt for my own sake and shall not call your sins to mind.

Isaiah 53:1–12   Ours were the sufferings he was bearing, ours the sorrows he was carrying . . . he was being wounded for our rebellions, crushed because of our guilt . . . we have been healed by his bruises.

Isaiah 55:1–11   Let [the sinner] turn back to Yahweh who will take pity . . . to our God, for he is rich in forgiveness.

Isaiah 58:1–11   If you deprive yourself for the hungry and satisfy the needs of the afflicted, your light will rise in the darkness, and your darkest hour will be like noon.

Isaiah 59:1–4, 9–15   The arm of Yahweh is not too short to save.

Jeremiah 2:1–13   My people have committed two crimes: they have abandoned me, the fountain of living water, and dug water-tanks for themselves, cracked water-tanks that hold no water.

Jeremiah 7:21–26   Listen to my voice, then I will be your God and you shall be my people.

Ezekiel 11:14–21   I shall remove the heart of stone from their bodies and give them a heart of flesh, so that they can keep my laws and respect my judgements and put them into practice.

Ezekiel 18:20–32   If the wicked, however, renounces all the sins he has committed . . . he will most certainly live; he will not die.

Ezekiel 36:23–28   I shall pour clean water over

you and you shall be cleansed; I shall cleanse you
of all your filth and of all your foul idols.

Hosea 2:16–25 I shall betroth you to myself in
loyalty and in the knowledge of Yahweh.

Hosea 11:1–11 I myself took them by the arm,
but they did not know that I was the one caring
for them.

Hosea 14:2–10 Israel, come back to Yahweh your
God.

Joel 2:12–19 "Come back to me with all your
heart."

Micah 6:1–4, 6–8 "You have already been told
what is right and what Yahweh wants of you.
Only this, to do what is right, to love loyalty and
to walk humbly with your God."

Zechariah 1:1–6 "Return to me, and I will return
to you."

READINGS FROM THE PSALMS

Psalm 12 Help, Yahweh! No one loyal is left.

Psalm 24 Who shall go up to the mountain of
Yahweh?

Psalm 30:1–6 Thanksgiving after mortal danger.

Psalm 31 Prayer in time of ordeal.

Psalm 35 Prayer of the virtuous in persecution.

Psalm 49:7–8, 14–23 No one can ever redeem
oneself.

Psalm 50 "Let thanksgiving be your sacrifice to
God."

Psalm 72   He has pity on the weak and the needy.

Psalm 89   A prayer to God the faithful.

Psalm 94   The God of justice.

Psalm 118:1, 10–13, 15–16   Give thanks to
  Yahweh for he is good.

Psalm 122   "Let us go to the house of Yahweh."

Psalm 130:3–4   We could not survive, except that
  God forgives us.

Psalm 139:1–18, 23–24   Your faithful love endures
  for ever, do not abandon what you have made.

Psalm 143:1–11   He brought back Israel's exiles,
  healing their broken hearts, and binding up their
  wounds.

READINGS FROM THE NEW TESTAMENT

Romans 3:22–26   All are justified by the free gift
  of his grace through being set free in Christ
  Jesus.

Romans 5:6–11   It is proof of God's own love for
  us, that Christ died for us while we were still
  sinners.

Romans 6:2b–13   See yourselves as being dead to
  sin but alive for God in Christ Jesus.

Romans 6:16–23   The wage paid by sin is death;
  the gift freely given by God is eternal life in
  Christ Jesus our Lord.

Romans 7:14–25   Who will rescue me . . . ?

God—thanks be to him—through Jesus Christ our Lord.

Romans 12:1–2, 9–19   Do not model your behavior on the contemporary world, but let the renewing of your minds transform you.

Romans 13:8–14   The only thing you should owe to anyone is love for one another, for to love the other person is to fulfill the law . . . Love can cause no harm to your neighbor . . . Let your armor be the Lord Jesus Christ.

2 Corinthians 5:17–21   [God] reconciled us to himself through Christ.

Galatians 5:16–24   All who belong to Christ Jesus have crucified self with all its passions and its desires.

Ephesians 2:1–10   But God, being rich in faithful love, through the great love with which he loved us even when we were dead through our sins, brought us to life with Christ.

Ephesians 4:1–3, 17–32   You must give up your old way of life.

Ephesians 5:1–14   You were darkness once, but now you are light in the Lord; behave as children of light.

Ephesians 6:10–18   Put on the full armor of God so as to be able to resist the devil's tactics.

Colossians 3:1–10, 12–17   Since you have been brought back to true life with Christ, you must look for the things that are in heaven.

Hebrews 12:1–5   In the fight against sin, you have

not yet had to keep fighting to the point of blood-shed.

James 1:22–27   You must do what the Word tells you, and not just listen to it and deceive your-selves.

James 2:14–26   Faith is expressed in good works.

James 3:1–12   Try to sanctify your speech.

1 Peter 1:13–23   The ransom paid to free you was paid by the precious blood of Jesus Christ.

2 Peter 1:3–11   The call and reward of christian living.

1 John 1:5–10; 2:1–2   If we say, "We have no sin," we are deceiving ourselves . . . but if anyone does sin, we have our advocate with the Father, Jesus Christ, the upright.

1 John 2:3–11   Whoever hates someone is still in darkness.

1 John 3:1–24   We have passed out of death into life because we love our brothers and sisters.

1 John 4:16–21   God is love, and whoever remains in love remains in God and God in him/her.

Revelation 2:1–5   You have less love now than for-merly . . . repent.

Revelation 3:14–22   Since you are neither hot nor cold, but only lukewarm, I will spit you out of my mouth.

Revelation 20:11–15   All were judged as their deeds deserved.

Revelation 21:1–8   Anyone who proves victorious will inherit these things; and I will be his/her God, and he/she will be my son/daughter.

READINGS FROM THE GOSPELS

Matthew 3:1–12 John the Baptist preached repentance for "the kingdom of Heaven is close at hand."

Matthew 4:12–17 Having overcome the temptation in the wilderness, Jesus began to preach: "Repent, for the kingdom of Heaven is close at hand."

Matthew 5:1–12 The Beatitudes.

Matthew 5:13–16 Your light must shine in people's sight.

Matthew 5:17–48 The one who keeps my commandments will be considered great in the kingdom of Heaven.

Matthew 9:1–8 The Cure of the Paralytic: "Take comfort, my child, your sins are forgiven."

Matthew 9:9–13 Call of Matthew: Jesus came to call sinners.

Matthew 18:15–20 Correcting brothers and sisters.

Matthew 18:21–35 Forgiving seventy times seven times.

Matthew 25:31–46 In so far as you did this to one of the least of these brothers/sisters of mine, you did it to me.

Matthew 26:69–75 Peter's denials.

Mark 12:28–34 The greatest commandment.

Luke 5:31–32 It is not those that are well who

need the doctor, but the sick. I have come to call
not the upright but sinners to repentance.

Luke 6:31–38 Love your enemies and do good.

Luke 7:36–50 The Woman Who Was a Sinner: her
sins, many as they are, have been forgiven her,
because she has shown such great love.

Luke 13:1–9 Examples inviting repentance.

Luke 15:1–10 Two parables of God's mercy: the
lost sheep and the lost drachma.

Luke 15:11–32 The Prodigal Son: While he was
still a long way off, his father saw him and was
moved with pity. He ran to the boy, clasped him
in his arms and kissed him.

Luke 17:1–6 If someone wrongs you seven times a
day and seven times comes back to you and says,
"I am sorry," you must forgive that person.

Luke 18:9–14 The Pharisee and the Publican:
"God, be merciful to me, a sinner."

Luke 19:1–10 The Story of Zacchaeus: The Son of
man has come to seek out and save what was
lost.

Luke 23:39–43 The Good Thief: "Today you will
be with me in paradise."

John 8:1–11 The Adulterous Woman: "Neither
do I condemn you," said Jesus. "Go away, and
from this moment sin no more."

John 8:31–36 Everyone who commits sin is a
slave.

John 15:1–8 Every branch that does bear fruit the
Father prunes to make it bear even more.

John 15:9–14   I call you friends.
John 19:13–37   The crucifixion of Jesus.
John 20:19–23   Receive the Holy Spirit. If you forgive anyone's sins, they are forgiven.

6 / HERE'S HOW IT'S DONE

EXAMINATION OF CONSCIENCE #1

There are many ways that an individual can examine his/her conscience. The key, of course, is to be honest with oneself. There is no need for fear as the Spirit reveals areas of sinfulness in our life. He brings things to the light so that the love of the Father may heal us with forgiveness.

In examining one's conscience, look for trends—areas in your life where you consistently have failed to live the life of Jesus, areas where you have failed to respond obediently to the Lord's call of service and mercy exemplified by Jesus himself, areas where you have consistently failed to respond to the Gospel's command of love. Always remember, however, that the main concern is to detect and acknowledge when we have not lived for God: chosen his love, his Kingdom, his Word as our guide and reference point.

By proceeding in this manner, you will, more than likely, notice that the Lord seems to work on a particular area, a bit at a time. We are, of course, completely forgiven when we confess our sins, yet the Spirit often leads us to focus on an area where our efforts, and his graces, might be given an opportunity to concentrate. Respond accordingly. If, for example, lust is the area of sinfulness, do not be surprised when it takes many different forms: lust for power, lust for drugs, food, sex, clothes, affirmation. Perhaps it will appear under the guise of knowledge as we throw ourselves into solving a problem, leaving relationships with friends and loved ones in our wake as we give the problem-solving all our time and energy. All of this stems from one sin with many different wrappings.

What follows is a form of examination of conscience offered in the *Rite of Penance,* Appendix III. Here the individual penitent is asked to consider the following questions when preparing for the celebration of the sacrament.

1. What is my attitude to the sacrament of penance? Do I sincerely want to be set free from sin, to turn again to God, to begin a new life, and to enter into a deeper friendship with God? Or do I look on it as a burden, to be undertaken as seldom as possible?

2. Did I forget to mention, or deliberately conceal, any grave sins in past confessions?

3. Did I perform the penance I was given? Did I make reparation for any injury to others? Have I tried to put into practice my resolution to lead a better life in keeping with the Gospel?

Next, the individual is encouraged to examine his/her life in the light of God's word.

I. The Lord says: "You shall love the Lord your God with your whole heart."

1. Is my heart set on God, so that I really love him above all things and am faithful to his commandments, as a son [daughter] loves his father? Or am I more concerned about the things of this world? Have I a right intention in what I do?

2. God spoke to us in his Son. Is my faith in God firm and secure? Am I wholehearted in accepting the Church's teaching? Have I been careful to grow in my understanding of the faith, to hear God's word, to listen to instructions on the faith, to avoid dangers to faith? Have I been always strong and fearless in professing my faith in God and the Church? Have I been willing to be known as a Christian in private and public life?

3. Have I prayed morning and evening? When I pray, do I really raise my mind and heart to God or is it a matter of words only? Do I offer God my difficulties, my joys, and my sorrows? Do I turn to God in time of temptation?

4. Have I love and reverence for God's name? Have I offended him in blasphemy, swearing falsely, or taking his name in vain? Have I shown disrespect for the Blessed Virgin Mary and the saints?

5. Do I keep Sundays and feast days holy by taking a full part, with attention and devotion, in the liturgy, and especially in the Mass? Have I ful-

filled the precept of annual confession and of communion during the Easter season?

6. Are there false gods that I worship by giving them greater attention and deeper trust than I give to God: money, superstition, spiritism, or other occult practices?

II. The Lord says: "Love one another as I have loved you."

1. Have I a genuine love for my neighbors? Or do I use them for my own ends, or do to them what I would not want done to myself? Have I given grave scandal by my words or actions?

2. In my family life, have I contributed to the well-being and happiness of the rest of the family by patience and genuine love? Have I been obedient to parents, showing them proper respect and giving them help in their spiritual and material needs? Have I been careful to give a Christian upbringing to my children, and to help them by good example and by exercising authority as a parent? Have I been faithful to my husband (wife) in my heart and in my relations with others?

3. Do I share my possessions with the less fortunate? Do I do my best to help the victims of oppression, misfortune, and poverty? Or do I look down on my neighbor, especially the poor, the sick, the elderly, strangers, and people of other races?

4. Does my life reflect the mission I received in confirmation? Do I share in the apostolic and charitable works of the Church and in the life of my parish? Have I helped to meet the needs of the

Church and of the world and prayed for them: for unity in the Church, for the spread of the Gospel among the nations, for peace and justice, etc.?

5. Am I concerned for the good and prosperity of the human community in which I live, or do I spend my life caring only for myself? Do I share to the best of my ability in the work of promoting human relations? Have I done my duty as a citizen? Have I paid my taxes?

6. In my work or profession am I just, hard-working, honest, serving society out of love for others? Have I paid a fair wage to my employees? Have I been faithful to my promises and contracts?

7. Have I obeyed legitimate authority and given it due respect?

8. If I am in a position of responsibility or authority, do I use this for my own advantage or for the good of others, in a spirit of service?

9. Have I been truthful and fair, or have I injured others by deceit, calumny, detraction, rash judgment, or violation of a secret?

10. Have I done violence to others by damage to life or limb, reputation, honor, or material possessions? Have I involved them in loss? Have I been responsible for advising an abortion or procuring one? Have I kept up hatred for others? Am I estranged from others through quarrels, enmity, insults, anger? Have I been guilty of refusing to testify to the innocence of another because of selfishness?

11. Have I stolen the property of others? Have I

desired it unjustly and inordinately? Have I damaged it? Have I made restitution of other people's property and made good their loss?

12. If I have been injured, have I been ready to make peace for the love of Christ and to forgive, or do I harbor hatred and the desire for revenge?

III. Christ our Lord says: "Be perfect as your Father is perfect."

1. Where is my life really leading me? Is the hope of eternal life my inspiration? Have I tried to grow in the life of the Spirit through prayer, reading the word of God and meditating on it, receiving the sacraments, self-denial? Have I been anxious to control my vices, my bad inclinations and passions, e.g., envy, love of food and drink? Have I been proud and boastful, thinking myself better in the sight of God and despising others as less important than myself? Have I imposed my own will on others, without respecting their freedom and rights?

2. What use have I made of time, of health and strength, of the gifts God has given me to be used like the talents in the Gospel? Do I use them to become more perfect every day? Or have I been lazy and too much given to leisure?

3. Have I been patient in accepting the sorrows and disappointments of life? How have I performed mortification so as to "fill up what is wanting to the sufferings of Christ"? Have I kept the precept of fasting and abstinence?

4. Have I kept my senses and my whole body pure and chaste as a temple of the Holy Spirit con-

secrated for resurrection and glory, and as a sign of
God's faithful love for men and women, a sign that
is seen most perfectly in the sacrament of matri-
mony? Have I dishonored my body by fornication,
impurity, unworthy conversation or thoughts, evil
desires, or actions? Have I given in to sensuality?
Have I indulged in reading, conversation, shows,
and entertainments that offend against Christian
and human decency? Have I encouraged others to
sin by my own failure to maintain these standards?
Have I been faithful to the moral law in my married
life?

5. Have I gone against my conscience out of fear
or hypocrisy?

6. Have I always tried to act in the true freedom
of the sons [and daughters] of God according to the
law of the Spirit, or am I the slave of forces within
me?

EXAMINATION OF CONSCIENCE #2

Though not technically an examination of conscience, the following prayer exercise will help the
individual keep track of the Spirit's movement on a
day-to-day basis. The examination of conscience offered in the *Rite of Penance* can easily take a long
period of time to complete. An individual may get
discouraged as he/she seems to answer negatively
to all the questions asked. Our sin can easily overwhelm us causing us to fall prey to the temptation

of the Evil One who tries to convince us that all is lost. By using the following prayer exercise, however, an individual can learn how to fine tune his/her heart to the promptings of the Spirit. It is not meant to help us see the right and wrong committed, but to sense the inner movements and promptings of the Spirit who has been directing us throughout the day. By learning how to sensitize ourselves to his presence, we will be able to recognize sin, avoid it when recognized, and know how to respond to a given situation with the heart and mind of Jesus. The whole process works best when kept to a maximum of fifteen minutes a day, just before we retire.

1. Relax. Know you are in God's presence. If desirable, sing a hymn, pray a psalm, or play a selection from a Christian music album.

2. Thank the Lord for everything he has brought into your life since the day before.

3. *Beg* to be given the mind and heart of Jesus, to see reality as Jesus sees it.

4. Reflect prayerfully over your day by checking the "we" (what you and Jesus experienced together) against the "I" (you alone). This is done in order to bring to life St. Paul's insight: "It is no longer I, but Christ living in me" (Ga 2:20). This means, of course, that our life is a "we" (you and Jesus) not an "I".

As you reflect over the day, visualize those events about which you can say "we" (even if you were not conscious of his presence at the time). For example, "We ate breakfast, we drove to work, we cleaned the house, we went to Mass, we helped in school, we spent time with the sick, etc."

Recall, then, those events about which you cannot say "we." For example, "I blew up at the children, I sat down and watched a sex movie, I got angry at the slow traffic, I cheated in the store, etc."

As you prayerfully review the day's events in this manner, the Spirit will make you aware of the myriad ways in which he was present to you through the day. He will enable you to "discern" or distinguish his touch from all the other movements, promptings, and urges in your life. This, in turn, will help you to become more aware of his presence in the days ahead. This awareness will evolve into that ideal of working, playing, resting, living in him that St. Paul describes.

5. Renew, in love, your sorrow for ever having disappointed or offended the Father. Offer a short prayer of repentance and sorrow at this time.

6. Plan a time of prayer for tomorrow. Make it definite in length and place. Also, promise to repair any damage you may have done to others should he give you the opportunity tomorrow.

7. End by praying the Our Father.

PRAYER OF THE PENITENT (ACT OF CONTRITION)

The Prayer of the Penitent offers the individual an opportunity to speak to the Lord from his/her heart. Unfortunately, many Catholics are ill at ease with this type of self-expression. If you find yourself in that situation, know that there are ways to overcome this; confront the situation directly. Begin by using times when you are alone so you might "practice" praying aloud. The prayers do not have to be long, or perfectly phrased; they do not have to be perfect in any sense of the word. Simply pray. The Lord knows us better than we can imagine. He will give us the words that best express our heartfelt sorrow.

In the past we used a form prayer for the Prayer of the Penitent. At that time it was called the Act of Contrition. What follows are several prayer examples offered in the *Rite of Penance,* 45, 85–92. Use them as they are given, namely as examples. Do not feel bound by them. They are there to help, not to hinder.

Remember that the best prayer is one that is sincere, not one that impresses the priest or shows off your ability to memorize. Proceed with confidence. The reward will be great.

My God,
I am sorry for my sins with all my heart.

In choosing to do wrong
and failing to do good,
I have sinned against you
whom I should love above all things.
I firmly intend, with your help,
to do penance,
to sin no more,
and to avoid whatever leads me to sin.
Our Savior Jesus Christ
suffered and died for us.
In his name, my God, have mercy.

Psalm 25:6–7
Remember, Lord, your compassion and mercy
which you showed long ago.
Do not recall the sins and failings of my youth.
In your mercy remember me, Lord, because of
your goodness.

Psalm 50:4–5
Wash me from my guilt
and cleanse me of my sin.
I acknowledge my offense;
my sin is before me always.

Luke 15:18; 18:13
Father, I have sinned against you
and am not worthy to be called your son
[daughter].
Be merciful to me, a sinner.

Father of mercy,
like the prodigal son
I return to you and say:
"I have sinned against you
and am no longer worthy to be called your son
[daughter]."
Christ Jesus, Savior of the world,
I pray with the repentant thief
to whom you promised Paradise:
"Lord, remember me in your kingdom."
Holy Spirit, fountain of love,
I call on you with trust:
"Purify my heart,
and help me to walk as a child of the light."

Lord Jesus,
you opened the eyes of the blind,
healed the sick,
forgave the sinful woman,
and after Peter's denial confirmed him in your
love.
Listen to my prayer:
forgive all my sins,
renew your love in my heart,
help me to live in perfect unity with my fellow
Christians
that I may proclaim your saving power to all the
world.

Lord Jesus,
you chose to be called the friend of sinners.

By your saving death and resurrection
free me from my sins.
May your peace take root in my heart
and bring forth a harvest
of love, holiness, and truth.

Lord Jesus Christ,
you are the Lamb of God;
you take away the sins of the world.
through the grace of the Holy Spirit
restore me to friendship with your Father,
cleanse me from every stain of sin
in the blood you shed for me,
and raise me to new life
for the glory of your name.

Lord God,
in your goodness have mercy on me:
do not look on my sins,
but take away all my guilt.
Create in me a clean heart
and renew within me an upright spirit.

Lord Jesus, Son of God,
have mercy on me, a sinner.

EXAMPLE OF THE CELEBRATION FOR AN INDIVIDUAL PENITENT

What follows is a sample dialogue for the celebration of reconciliation with an individual penitent. Needless to say, this is meant as an example only. It is not intended to dictate what should or must be said by either the penitent or the priest. The situation which is fabricated in this dialogue involves a married man, age thirty-four, who has been away from the sacraments since college.

Reception of the Penitent

PRIEST   (Welcoming the penitent into the reconciliation room, the priest extends his hand in greeting.) Hello! I'm Father Chris. Please make yourself comfortable. You can sit beside me, or, if you prefer, kneel at the prie-dieu.

PENITENT   (Feeling a bit uncomfortable since he had not been to the sacrament in a while) Hello, Father. Things sure have changed since I went to confession last. I'm not quite sure what to do. Will you please help me? Do I kneel, or sit? I don't know if I even remember any of the prayers I'm suppose to say.

PRIEST   (Trying to make the penitent feel comfortable and relaxed, despite his obvious discomfort) The best way to begin is to place ourselves under

God's sign of protection. Don't worry about your unfamiliarity with the "new way" the sacrament is celebrated. Let's just move through this together, so you can experience and receive all that the Lord desires for you. Let's bless ourselves, therefore, and place ourselves under the Lord's sign of victory.

PRIEST AND PENITENT (Making the sign of the cross together) In the name of the Father, and of the Son, and of the Holy Spirit. Amen.

PRIEST (Inviting the penitent to trust in the Lord) My brother, may the Lord now fill you with the Spirit so that fear is removed from your inner being, freeing you to confess with confidence in the Lord's mercy.

Reading of the Word of God

PRIEST If I may, I would like to begin with a short scripture verse. I know you may be unfamiliar with this, but it is important that we place ourselves within the proper frame of mind. I know of no better way than recalling what the Lord tells us through his holy word. If you have a favorite passage, I would be glad to use that one. If not, I'll chose one of my favorites.

PENITENT Funny you should ask, Father. But I do have a favorite passage. I know I have not been to the sacraments in a long time, but God has still been very real to me. In fact, the reason I came here was because I heard this passage while

I was switching radio stations! I don't know where it is, but, perhaps, you may know. It's the story where Jesus asks Peter if he loves him.

PRIEST I'm sure I can locate that one, if you give me a moment. Yes, here it is in St. John's Gospel, chapter 21, verses 15–19. Would you like to read it?

PENITENT No, Father. I would prefer if you did, if you don't mind.

PRIEST Certainly not. Before reading it, however, let's spend a moment in quiet prayer, asking the Lord to open our hearts to what he wants us to hear through this reading. (Both pause before the priest reads the text, and again after the text is read.) What do you hear the Lord saying?

PENITENT It's all a jumble, Father. All I know is that when I heard this on the radio, I knew I had to speak to someone who could help me. I want very much to love the Lord, and yet I've been distant from the Church for such a long time. When I hear the words "Do you love me?" I want to answer with Peter, "Lord, you know I love you." That's why I came to confession.

PRIEST It's obvious that the Lord has touched you and desires to grace you with a clean heart and renewed spirit. There's a great deal for which you can be grateful, not only that he's been calling you, but that you have been able to respond. Let's proceed with confidence, therefore, knowing that the Lord has led you here precisely so you can be freed from your sins and given the opportunity to start anew within his Church.

PENITENT Yes, Father, that's just what I want to do.

Confession of Sins and Acceptance of Penance

PRIEST Okay, then, trusting in the Lord's mercy and love, I invite you to confess your sins.

PENITENT Father, it's been so long since my last confession, I don't even know where to begin.

PRIEST Well, how long is "so long."

PENITENT It's been a good number of years. I haven't gone to confession or communion since I got married. That was almost ten years ago. I had just finished college, was looking for a job, and really did not have any time for God.

PRIEST I know it will be hard for you to remember everything that has occurred in the last ten years, so let's look at the trends in your life and see how you may have responded to or disobeyed the Spirit of God. (At this point, the priest leads the penitent in a brief examination of conscience, focusing on his responsibility as a married man to his wife and his children. Has he been loving and faithful, a gentle father, honest at work, a good neighbor, etc.?)

PENITENT As you can see, Father, I haven't really done anything that is really bad. I just haven't done anything that truly kept me close to God. I see now that my decisions seldom had him in mind; they usually had only me. Even my wife and kids weren't the center of my life. I always tried to please myself first, though I made it look as if I had their interests at heart. I know why that reading had such a profound effect on me. It was God asking me directly whether or not I really loved him, whether or not I would really let him love me.

PRIEST   I think you have only started to hear all that the Lord wants to say to you. There will be much more. Remember his love is forever, and his love is unlimited. The more you yield to that love, the more you will experience his working in your life. There should be little doubt in your mind that the Lord forgives your sins. He brought you to this point precisely so you can know that forgiveness. As a sign of your willingr.ess to respond, I am going to request that you do a penance.

PENITENT   I'll do anything you want, Father. I admit, though, I may not know a prayer you give me to say. It's been a long time, you know.

PRIEST   I wasn't thinking of asking you to say a particular prayer. I was thinking of an action which would open your heart even further to what the Lord desires to tell you.

PENITENT   Sounds good to me. What is it?

PRIEST   I would like you to attend the parish mission which is beginning next week. We have it every Advent season, in preparation for Christmas. The speakers are really excellent: a priest, a layman, and a laywoman. Attending the mission will give you additional time to hear God tell you he loves you.

PENITENT Father, I remember missions from when I was a kid. They usually last an entire week, don't they?

PRIEST Yes, they usually do. Ours, in fact, will be offered in the morning and the evening from Monday through Thursday.

PENITENT Father, I really want to say yes, but I know I could not go on each of those nights. I've already promised my son to take him to a football game on Tuesday. Would it be all right if I went the other days, and missed Tuesday?

PRIEST Of course. I don't want you to see the penance as something you owe God to pay for your sins. See it as an opportunity to place yourself in a position where God can continue to change your life. By all means, come on Monday to the opening session of the mission, and then finish up on Wednesday and Thursday if you find it helpful. I'm pretty sure you will.

PENITENT I'll gladly do that, Father.

Prayer of the Penitent

PRIEST Now let's take a few moments and pray together. You pray the Act of Contrition, and I'll pray for you at the same time.

PENITENT Father, I don't think I can say the entire Act of Contrition. I really don't remember it all.

PRIEST That's okay. Speak from your heart. There's no need for you to focus on a foggy memory; focus instead on what you're feeling inside. Use the words that allow you to be comfortable.

PENITENT That's certainly different from what I remember. I'll try. (Penitent pauses for a moment with head bowed.) Dear God, I'm really sorry for being away from you so long. I know you were never away from me. There's a lot of catching up I have to do: loving you, my family, my kids a bit better. I know I can't do it without you. Please help me. I promise to try my best to follow you. Forgive me for the times I did not even think about you. Help me. I want to love you more.

Absolution

PRIEST Heavenly Father, I praise and thank you for sending your Son into our world so we can know you better. Allow that Spirit which is your gift to us to fill the heart of my brother, who has come to seek your mercy and love. Grant him his heart's desire: to love you more completely. I thank you for drawing him to you after these many years. I thank you for using the simple moments of his life to speak your word of invitation to him. Keep him ever open to that word. (Standing over the penitent, the priest places his hands

on the penitent's head.) My brother, remember
that God, the Father of mercies, through the
death and resurrection of his Son has reconciled
the world to himself and sent the Holy Spirit
among us for the forgiveness of sins; through the
ministry of the Church may God give you pardon and peace, and I absolve you from your sins
in the name of the Father, and of the Son, † and
of the Holy Spirit.

PENITENT   Amen.

Proclamation of Praise of God and Dismissal

PRIEST   The Lord has freed you from sin. May he
bring you safely to his kingdom in heaven. Glory
to him for ever.

PENITENT   Amen.

PRIEST   (Placing his hand upon the penitent's
shoulder, the priest continues to talk with the
penitent as they move toward the exit of the reconciliation room.) Remember that this is just the
beginning for you. The Lord has spent some time
getting your attention so you can respond to his
invitation. Keep your ears and heart open to his
voice.

PENITENT   I will, Father. And thanks a lot for
helping me. It may be different from what I remember, but it sure seems better. Thanks again,
Father. (Both shake hands.)

7 / PRAYER EXERCISES FOR INNER HEALING

The following thoughts on inner healing are by no means complete. They are presented to the reader as an offer and challenge to pursue the fullness of God's promise within his/her life. At best, these paragraphs outline in a cursory fashion the experience of many lay people and religious who have come to know not only the forgiveness of their sins, but the healing of their inner spirit. Several books have already been mentioned in the text. To obtain a better understanding of this prayer experience, I would again recommend these books to you.

As mentioned in the text, individuals who celebrate the Sacrament of Reconciliation often find themselves in need of further prayer. This additional prayer does not deal with the forgiveness of sin, but with the healing of inner hurts caused by sin. We already know and believe that Jesus, through his death and resurrection, reconciles all to himself. This reconciliation, celebrated in the sacrament, is meant to unfold in every aspect of our lives, in the very quality of life we experience in the Spirit. It is inner healing which helps to integrate this fact of reconciliation so that true life is added to our days.

Because the effects of sin are so pervasive and deep, we who are forgiven often remain burdened by depression, poor self-images, inferiority complexes, unreasonable fears and anxieties, psychosomatic illnesses, etc. Jesus, however, has come "to proclaim liberty to captives . . . to let the oppressed go free" (Lk 4:18). He intends, through his offer of reconciliation, to make the whole person new. As St. Paul rightly exclaims: "So for anyone who is in Christ, there is a new creation: the old order is gone and a new being is there to see" (2 Co 5:17).

Relationships, therefore, that had bent our inner heart out of shape because love was lost or trust betrayed can now be renewed in the "new creation" that is Christ. The effects of social and systemic sin, nurturing within us the lie that caused the original sin rather than the truth of our sonship/daughtership, can now be rooted out. The effect of others' sins, which often harden us in defensive stances (see Paul's corporate vision of the inner working of the Body, 1 Co 12f), can now be defused, rendering them powerless. All this occurs because Jesus desires to lift not only our sins but our burdens, to take past memories and heal them, along with the resulting wounds which still affect us.

In speaking of this experience, however, one must distinguish between inner healing and spiritual growth. Father Michael Scanlan in his work

Inner Healing (New York: Paulist Press, 1974, p. 5), offers the following insight: "Healing is something distinct from growth or a qualitative improvement. Healing means the process by which what is wounded or sick becomes whole or healthy." This process is not necessarily a miracle, which involves an obvious change that cannot be explained, but a "naturally induced process to health" which can be known by faith alone. The main barrier to this process, according to Father Scanlan (p. 42), is our lack of forgiveness; the main catalyst, our willingness to trust, which, we have seen, is the basic stance of a true son/daughter of God.

It is often said that "seeing is believing." In order, therefore, to help us see more clearly the work of inner healing in our own life, the reader is invited to inspect the process of inner healing in the life of a familiar biblical person, Peter. Read, therefore, the accounts of Peter's denial, beginning with the arrest of Jesus in the Garden. The following texts will help you situate the scene: Matthew 26:47–75; Luke 22:47–62; and John 21:1–18.

Simon Peter: An Inner Healing Case Study

The scene does not take us by surprise: once again Peter had separated himself from the Master. It was not the first time (cf. Mt 16:21), and was probably not the last; his best foot forward often left him "at a distance" (see Mt 26:58). Regarding his emotions, there is little left to the imagination.

The scriptures make it perfectly clear: frustration, anger, despair. Jesus, who always had the quick answer, the right word, was strangely silent. Peter, however, could not remain silent; once again, he speaks out when *he* should have been the silent one. Oaths, curses, swearing spring from his lips (see Mt 26:74) and then, suddenly, his heart is pierced as he hears the cock crow. The moment is tersely framed in the Gospel (Mt 26:75): "And Peter remembered what Jesus had said, 'Before the cock crows you will have disowned me three times.' And he went outside and wept bitterly."

Peter's "sin" had hurt him at the deepest part of his being. The Lord, however, had already prayed for him (see Lk 22:31f) and knew that his "sin" would become an opportunity for God's grace to be victorious. To see this, we must move to John's post-resurrection accounts. Remember: according to John's account, Jesus had already revealed himself to the disciples at the time of his appearance by the Sea of Tiberias (see Jn 21:14) and had already sent the Spirit (see Jn 20). This appearance, therefore, was not simply revelatory. There was something else that had to be done to this "rock" upon whom the Church would be built. And so, Jesus went precisely to the place where Peter hung out— the fishing hole. Note what the account says: there is a large haul of fish, reminiscent of Peter's own call (see Mt 4:18–20) where it is promised that he will become a fisher of men; there is the threefold query, "Do you love me?" offsetting the threefold denial which had taken place in the courtyard; there is the recommissioning of Peter when he is told, "Feed my sheep." By remembering and "reliving," in Jesus' resurrected presence, the experience of call and denial and commissioning, Peter is revived spiritually and relationally.

And so it is with us. We too may find it beneficial to remember and "relive" our experiences of separation so that the presence of the resurrected Lord can revive us spiritually and relationally. It must be emphasized that this does not effect the forgiveness of sin, but soothes and heals the inner hurts caused by sin.

In the following section, two possible prayer methods are explained briefly. Either of these prayer exercises might be done alone, with a small group, or with one other person.

Using Imagination Prayer for Inner Healing

This is a relatively simple prayer exercise which many have found helpful in the process of inner healing. There is, of course, nothing "magical" involved, just an openness of heart which invites the ever-present power of Jesus' Spirit to move within us in a particular way.

As with any type of prayer, placing oneself in the proper frame of mind is important. Relax; be comfortable; breathe slowly and rhythmically. You may find it helpful to fix your attention on a religious symbol: a cross, an open Bible, a candle, etc. Ask the Spirit to come and prepare your heart for the Lord's coming. Use your own words; do not be afraid of how it sounds. We are not writing poetry but praying from the heart.

Even before entering into prayer, you may know the area where healing is needed. Perhaps the pain's origin had been obvious for a while; or, maybe you have just realized it, having been given an insight through the grace of reconciliation. You may, however, be totally unaware of the area that needs healing. Do not let this dissuade you. Within the experience of prayer, the Lord can reveal the origin, as well as heal the hurt.

If you already know the area where the Lord intends to work, then prepare to meet him there. As you quiet your inner spirit, imagine the scene where the hurt was experienced. Perhaps it was a harmful action you had done, or a hurt done to you. "Go back" into the scene, asking the Lord to enter it with you. If you had performed the hurtful action, ask the Lord to protect the person you injured. Imagine how Jesus might do this, and thank him for being there to protect the one you had harmed through your words or actions. As this is occurring, ask the Lord to show you *why* you had acted in such a way. More often than not, we hurt an individual because he/she has hurt us in some way. As Jesus shows you the root cause of your action and attitude toward the individual, ask him to heal you of your hurt, the hurt which compelled you to hurt another child of God. During this time, allow Jesus to console you and comfort you. Imagine how he would do this. Would he embrace you? or dry your tears? or walk silently next to you? Now ask Jesus to help you forgive the person you had injured, just as Jesus forgives you. If you were not the doer of the hurtful action, but the recipient, pray that the Lord protect you during that time. Let him stand between you and the individual(s) who had harmed you. Once again, ask for the grace to forgive those who had hurt you.

All this is possible because Jesus is our never-ending beginning. For him there is no time. He, therefore, is able "to enter" into our past (present or future), which is his always. "Imagining" that he is there during a past experience, therefore, is really not imagining at all! He *is* there, we simply did not perceive him. In prayer, however, through the grace of the Spirit, our perception can be renewed and refined. That which was unseen, can now, in faith, be seen, experienced, and known.

Such a prayer exercise can last an indefinite length of time. It depends on the Lord, and the way he chooses to heal us. He never does more mending than we are able to handle at a particular time. Remember, as human beings we need to process our experiences so they are integrated into our lives. This is certainly true of God's grace and loving kindness. When we sense, therefore, that the Lord is finished for the moment, begin to "return" from your prayer of imagination. End with a time of thanksgiving and praise. Perhaps a psalm or

Christian hymn may be helpful. I have found that the Lord's Prayer is an especially fruitful way of bringing such prayer times to a close.

Using Scripture Prayer for Inner Healing

The Word of God is an especially helpful tool as we seek to experience inner healing. This is because sacred scripture has a power that stands apart from our imagination and intellect; it is something "alive and active," seeking out "the place where the soul is divided from spirit," judging "secret emotions and thoughts" (Heb 4:12). It is, in fact, the Word of Life, treasured by the Church as God's own Word to us. By reflecting on this Word, therefore, the Lord is able to move powerfully in our inner being.

Using scripture for inner healing is similar in format to that of Imagination Prayer. Now, however, one starts with a particular scripture passage which is read several times. You may find it helpful to read it aloud, as well as silently. Next, imagine the scene just read. Visualize yourself standing on the perimeter of the picture. Now ask the Lord who you are to be in the scene. When you hear him invite you to "take part," do so. See yourself within the picture, and allow the scene to run its course.

Although this type of prayer is framed by the scriptural text, do not hesitate to follow the lead of the Spirit as you enter into the dialogue. What is Jesus saying to you? For example, when reading the passage about the Prodigal Son (see Lk 15:11–32), you may be invited to be one of the children in the story. There you may discover your own hurt and anger at being a child who is seemingly spurned by a father's love. The Lord, upon revealing such an insight to you, can bring about a very deep healing of father/child relationships, or brother/sibling relationships, etc.

For those who desire further reading on this subject, please refer to the books already mentioned in the text. In addition, Eddie Ensley's book, *Prayer That Heals Our Emotions* (Columbus, Ga.: Contemplative Books, 1986), may be helpful.

Before concluding this section, I would like to emphasize that prayer for inner healing is more than a Freudian exercise in uncovering the unconscious. It is a faith stance the believer lives because he/she knows that in Jesus Christ we are indeed made new. Note also that particular, written prayers have not been offered. Instead, a method was explained thereby empowering each individual to move in the direction that suits him/her best. Too often individual prayers are seen as magic formulae which must be said, word for word, to gain the desired result. Nothing could be further from the truth with inner healing prayer.

8 / QUESTIONS AND ANSWERS

The following questions and answers are in no particular order, having been gathered during many conversations with people who are striving to understand more deeply the Sacrament of Reconciliation. Even though some of the answers can be discovered throughout the text, it was decided to incorporate them into a chapter so that the reader will not have to hunt through many pages in order to find the answer to a particular question.

Please remember, however, that a Question and Answer section may help or hinder the one seeking an answer. The possibility for misunderstanding an answer that is presented in a short, non-documented form is a very real danger. I wish to acknowledge, therefore, that the answers presented merely skim the surface. Oftentimes, there may be more than one possible answer to the question, yet only one answer is given. This is not meant to eliminate or ignore the fact that other opinions might also be acceptable.

Q. Does the secrecy of the confessional still apply?
A. A priest is bound to secrecy within the confes-

sional. Sins, mentioned within the context of celebrating the sacrament, will not be revealed to anyone; confidentiality here is of the highest order (see Canon 983). The priest will neither refer to your sins, nor recall your sins to anyone.

Q. When did confessional screens originate?
A. In the tenth century, St. Charles Borromeo introduced them in order to protect the penitent from undue pressure or harassment.

Q. If a priest is not available, how can I receive forgiveness?
A. If a priest is unavailable, one should pray the Prayer of the Penitent, traditionally called an Act of Contrition. Trust in the Lord's mercy and love, and, if grave sin is involved, make every effort to receive the sacrament as soon as you are able.

Q. How can one experience the Sacrament of Reconciliation in areas where there is no priest, such as Third World countries, rural areas, etc.?
A. In such situations, the Church allows general absolution to be given. In this way, the traveling missionary can help the people celebrate the sacrament even when individual confession is an impossibility.

Q. Should a person have a steady confessor?
A. Many individuals find it fruitful to have one confessor over a period of time, though this is not required. Face-to-face confession is very rewarding in such cases.

Q. If a person who was away from the sacrament for a long time goes to confession but cannot remember all his/her sins, what should be done?

A. Those who are away from the sacrament for many years cannot be expected to remember all their sins. To do so would indicate a phenomenal ability to recall the past. However, there are, undoubtedly, areas of major concern that have not been forgotten. These should be confessed. In addition, indicating your sorrow for all forgotten sins of the past is encouraged. Having received the grace of the sacrament, do not be surprised if the Spirit of God brings to your mind those sins which you were unable to remember in the confessional. This is not unusual. Remember that those sins have already been forgiven and need not be confessed again. Nevertheless, prayer may still be sought so that inner healing can continue. Examples of such prayer exercises will be found in chapter 7.

Q. I received general absolution at a Lenten penance service. May I receive it again at the Advent service which is scheduled?

A. If grave sin is involved, an individual must first confess them to a priest before receiving general absolution again.

Q. Is it possible to have general absolution at Sunday Mass?

A. General absolution is not meant to be celebrated at Sunday Mass. If circumstances, for example, in mission areas, require it, general absolution may be permitted. More than likely it would not be done during Mass, but at a separate liturgical service. The norm, however, is to celebrate the sacrament within the context of individual confession.

Q.   In the past, frequent confession was encouraged. Today many priests seem to frown on it. How often should I receive the sacrament?

A.   The Church instructs us to celebrate the Sacrament of Reconciliation once a year if grave sin is involved. Traditionally the time for this is from Ash Wednesday to Trinity Sunday, thereby incorporating the Lenten and Easter seasons. Many people find devotional confessions helpful for spiritual growth and, therefore, seek the sacrament on a monthly basis. As mentioned in the text, this situation appears confusing to some since the same rite is used to reconcile those with grave sins as well as to assist those seeking to deepen their penitential lifestyle.

Q.   Can I receive the Sacrament of Reconciliation while Mass is being said?

A.   The Church does not encourage us to celebrate the Sacrament of Reconciliation while other liturgical celebrations, such as Eucharist, are taking place. There are times, however, when the priest is only available immediately before Mass. This is especially true in mission areas. Although not ideal, one should utilize the time that is available. But do not come five minutes before Mass and expect to celebrate the sacrament in a way that is uplifting and personalized. If time forces one to rush through the rite, the beauty and power of the celebration is easily lost.

Q.   Who can receive the Sacrament of Reconciliation?

A.   Any baptized Catholic has the right to celebrate the Sacrament of Reconciliation. With that right, however, goes the responsibility to accept the grace of the sacrament so that true conversion can take hold of our lives.

Q.   Where can the Sacrament of Reconciliation be celebrated?

A.   Any place, any time, anywhere. The church's reconciliation room is, of course, the usual place to celebrate the Sacrament of Reconciliation. Circumstances may dictate otherwise, for example, on battlefields, in hospitals, at scenes of accidents, etc. Most parishes have scheduled times to receive the sacrament. If these are not convenient, do not hesitate to contact a priest for an appointment. Remember, the new rite assumes that the celebration will take more than a few brief moments.

Q.   My friend is divorced and remarried, yet continues to go to communion. She said that the priest gave her permission in the "internal forum." What does this mean?

A.   For pastoral reasons, an individual may be permitted to receive the sacraments despite what appear to be valid reasons against it. These cases are called "internal forum" because they deal with details and information of which the public has no knowledge. Such cases are not meant to be an excuse for living a life that appears contrary to Gospel teaching. Rather, it is an opportunity for the Church to make the exception which, in fact, proves the rule.

It should also be noted that a priest does not give "permission" for an individual to act contrary to Church law or Gospel norms. Rather, through prayerful listening and direction, the priest may assist an individual in coming to determine the person's maximum response-ability in applying the Gospel to his/her present life.

Q. Should a person celebrate the Sacrament of Reconciliation even when he/she knows that change is not possible, for example, in cases of remarriage when an annulment has not yet been granted?
A. In such cases, it would be helpful to speak with the priest who has been assisting you in spiritual growth. Although "internal forum" solutions exist in certain difficult situations, one cannot make a general statement that covers all conditions.

Q. Is it necessary to itemize my sins?
A. The Council of Trent stated that sins must be itemized according to number and kind. This was necessary since many priests had to refer to penitential books in order to offer a proper penance for the sins confessed. In our present situation, stating the number of times, and the kinds of sins commit-

ted, is still encouraged because it helps to pinpoint the areas where conversion is needed. However, upon a careful examination of conscience, the individual will probably recognize that the number and kinds of sins confessed point to trends of sinfulness. Look for these trends of sin so they may be overcome.

Q.   *Whatever happened to the Act of Contrition?*
A.   The Act of Contrition is alive and well. In the new rite it is called the Prayer of the Penitent. Though the name is changed, the purpose remains the same: the expression of heartfelt sorrow. Use whatever words you desire, memorize one of the prayers offered in the rite, or write your own Prayer of the Penitent and bring it into the reconciliation room. Examples of such prayers are found in chapter 7.

Q.   *Are penances in the form of repetitive prayers still given?*
A.   The Church encourages that the type of penance given be "suitable to the personal condition of the penitent so that each one may restore the order which he disturbed and through the corresponding remedy be cured of the sickness from which he [she] suffered" *(Rite of Penance,* 6). Repetitive prayers, therefore, may not always be the best remedy for sin; actions speak louder than words.

Q.   *How do I make a good examination of conscience?*

A. See chapter 6.

Q. *When we are physically ill, we go to a doctor who specializes in that illness. Should I go to a priest whom I know will understand my sinfulness?*

A. The faithful are encouraged to seek a confessor who will assist them in any way whatsoever. One does not have to go to the parish priest.

Q. *If we have not committed serious sin, how often would we need to receive the sacrament?*

A. The Sacrament of Reconciliation should be celebrated at least once a year if serious sin is involved. Remember, however, that penance is a life-style for the believer. There are many ways that the Christian is encouraged to participate and celebrate that reality, for example, communal penance services.

Note also that one does not so much "receive" the sacrament as if it were a thing, but *celebrates* the sacrament which is a manifestation of God's loving kindness toward all.

Q. *If you go to confession and find yourself with a non-sympathetic or non-understanding priest, are you free to seek another who may be able to understand your problem better?*

A. Yes. However, be careful that you do not deceive yourself. Sometimes we want to "shop around" for a priest who agrees with our lifestyle rather than submit to a priest who may be proclaiming the Lord's Gospel to us.

Q. Should a child or an adult who is retarded receive the Sacrament of Reconciliation?
A.   This is one of those questions that has no easy answer. As mentioned in the text, the Sacrament of Reconciliation appears to be, on one hand, for those who have been separated from the community and are now seeking reconciliation and unity again. However, it is also encouraged for those who are seeking a deeper wallk with the Lord. Though a child or adult who is retarded cannot break his/her relationship with God in the same way that a healthy adult can, he/she can deepen his/her relationship with the Lord. We do not, however, have any official rite that takes this into consideration. Penance services prepared for these exceptional cases might be a way for such individuals to acknowledge personal and corporate sinfulness in a manner that is understandable to them, and to experience the acceptance of God's love.

Q. How can I be sure that my sins are forgiven?
A.   We are sure that our sins are forgiven in the same way we are sure of the Lord's presence in the Eucharist—faith.

Q. What happens if I do not do my penance?
A.   Penances are meant to be a remedy for sin. If one deliberately refuses to perform the penance that was given, the person's sincerity and sorrow could be questioned. Remember that the penitent has the opportunity during the celebration of the sacrament to state whether the penance is acceptable.

Q. When did the sacrament of confession become the Sacrament of Reconciliation?

A. In 1973, with the promulgation of the *Rite of Penance,* the official nomenclature was changed. Note that the rite itself often interchanges the phrases Sacrament of Reconciliation and Sacrament of Penance. This, quite naturally, tends to confuse the situation. Other phrases often used by commentators are "Sacrament of Peace" and "Sacrament of Healing Forgiveness." To my mind, the latter seems the best choice.

Q. Why is it not called the Sacrament of Penance?

A. Penance, according to the Church's tradition, is the lifestyle of the believer. Reconciliation is the term used to describe the process of reuniting, with the Church and with the Father, the one who has broken away.

Q. Does a priest have to be present to receive the sacrament?

A. A priest must be present to celebrate the Sacrament of Reconciliation as a liturgical sacramental event. However, a priest does not have to be present to experience the forgiveness of the Lord.

Q. Why should we bother going to the sacrament if a priest is not needed for receiving forgiveness? Why not just confess our sins to God?

A. Remember that the celebration of the sacrament is a communal affair. It is not a one-to-one, me-and-God-alone experience. Sin always has social overtones. In addition, we who are baptized into Christ Jesus are also united to one another by the very fact of our baptism. Not to be forgotten is the very act of "confessing," in which the sacrament is seen as a public form of praise and worship: by confessing our sins with faith in God's forgiveness, we are also "confessing" our praise and worship of a loving God.

Q. What are the benefits of the sacrament other than forgiveness of sins?

A.   Those who through daily weakness succumb to less serious sin, that is, venial sin, are able to draw strength from the celebration of the Sacrament of Reconciliation so they might gain the full freedom of the children of God. This freedom enables the individual to live a life of trust: trust in the Father's love; trust that he gifts us with his Spirit even when circumstances appear otherwise; trust that our sorrow will be turned to joy as we come to know him personally.

Coming to full freedom as a child of God provides us with the heartfelt exhilaration of knowing we are loved by Love. In like manner, this freedom generates a deep, inner peace as we accept ourselves because God accepts us, totally and completely. Release from fear, anxiety, anger, and bitterness are further characteristics of this freedom. In short, the freedom of God's children, offered and received as a gift, become more concrete in our lives as we enter fully into the process of reconciliation. Chapter 7, "Prayer Exercises for Inner Healing," offers additional thoughts on this topic.

In addition, the Sacrament of Reconciliation gives the individual the opportunity to conform more closely to Christ and to follow the voice of the Spirit more attentively by striving to perfect the grace of baptism so that, as we bear in our body the death of Jesus Christ, his life may be seen in us ever more clearly *(Rite of Penance, 7)*. In short, the sacrament helps us enter more fully into the dying/rising cycle of Jesus' paschal mystery.

Q. *Must a child go to confession before receiving First Holy Communion?*
A. There is a great deal of discussion regarding this matter. Canon Law states that those who have committed a grave sin must receive the Sacrament of Reconciliation. Nevertheless, many responsible members of the Church contend that this is not applicable to a child, although a child can most certainly commit sin. The Congregation for the Faith, however, says that children should receive the Sacrament of Reconciliation before receiving First Communion. Here, then, is the dilemma.

In answering the question, one can say for certain that an individual believer (young or old) who is guilty of serious sin is obliged to celebrate the Sacrament of Reconciliation during the course of the year. In some areas, celebration of the sacrament takes place before First Communion; in other areas, penance services are used to help the child experience and celebrate God's forgiveness; in still other areas, the Sacrament of Reconciliation is postponed until after First Communion. Because of this pastoral diversity, it will be important for the Church to continue clarifying the issue lest the focus of the sacrament become lost or confused.

Q.   If scripture says that our sins are forgiven and forgotten, why does the Church teach there is a purgatory?

A.   Scripture encourages us to pray for the dead (cf. 2 M 12:44–45). It was in attempting to respond to this passage that the idea of purgatory developed. As with any technical, theological phrase, an understanding of the particular philosophical system that was operating at the time is important. When this is done, purgatory takes on its proper meaning.

The term itself arose during the Middle Ages to describe the purifying growth of perfection needed in all the dimensions of our human life. This purification was considered necessary so the debt of punishment incurred by sin might be paid. This is not to say that forgiveness had not been given. Rather, purgatory was seen as a purification process needed to remove the effects of sin.

Q.   Whatever happened to limbo?

A.   There is no official teaching regarding the idea of limbo. Originally, the term arose from the idea of *sheol* in Later Judaism, and became especialy widespread in the Scholastic period. As with the term purgatory, the phrase must be placed in the proper historical context in order to be understood. Since that context has changed, the term does not have the same import as it did during the Scholastic period.

Q. *Is there a hell?*

A. The Church teaches that those who have willingly and deliberately turned from God would be assigned to an eternity without him. This "place" is called hell. One must not, however, think in terms of a geographic location. Rather, view it as an attempt to picture that state of being where God is not accepted by the individual.

Q. *What should you do when you are sincerely looking for spiritual growth, but the priest takes your confession casually, or tells you not to come back?*

A. Seek a confessor who will help you. Do not, however, deceive yourself: the priest *may* be offering advice you need to hear. If, for example, a penitent continues to confess the same sins but does not make any effort to overcome them, the priest may understandably ask that person to come to the sacrament less frequently, but to strive more deliberately to overcome the sins confessed. Another instance might arise when an individual incorrectly determines and judges the gravity of a certain action or actions. In such cases, the priest may be trying to show the individual that such actions are not matter for confession.

Q. Matthew 16:19 tells us "Whatever you bind on earth will be bound in heaven . . ." Does the "you" refer only to the priest standing in the place of Jesus?
A.   Each of us, in a sense, has the power to bind a person by our lack of forgiveness. If we refuse to forgive our enemies, we have, in fact, bound them. Our lack of forgiveness, therefore, can be a barrier for their growth in the Spirit. In a formal, communal way, a priest has the power, through the ministry of the Church, to bind and loose our sins.

Q.   I have often heard the term "fundamental option." Please explain.
A.   This is a technical term used in contemporary moral theology to express the overall orientation an individual has toward or away from God. The point of the phrase is to show that our relationship with God does not deteriorate with one serious sin.

Q.   What is the sin against the Holy Spirit?
A.   Scripture speaks about the "sin against the Holy Spirit" in Matthew 12:31f and Mark 3:28f where the passage is placed in the context of Jesus' casting out demons, and the criticism leveled against him by the Pharisees who refuse to believe. It is also stated in Luke 12:10 immediately following the section that calls people to be public witnesses of the Son of Man. The phrase remains cryptic in that it does not say what the "sin against the Spirit" might be. There has been no official teaching on the matter, although speculation abounds. It would appear that the sin of which Jesus speaks

might be the sin of denying the Spirit's power and purpose: the power to sanctify and the purpose of drawing all men and women into unity with the Father and the Son. Others would say that the sin is a denial of Jesus' Lordship, which is what the Spirit proclaims within us. In the encyclical *Dominum et Vivificantem,* 46, John Paul II offers this further insight: "Blasphemy against the Holy Spirit, then, is the sin committed by the person who claims to have a 'right' to persist in evil—in any sin at all— and who thus rejects redemption."

Q. Are sins still mortal or venial?
A. The terms mortal and venial sins arise from the Scholastic system of theology which was operative during the Council of Trent. Many theologians today use other terms to express human sinfulness. In some ways the categories mortal and venial are useful, in that certain actions can be neatly classified. However, an unhealthy legalism can also arise.

When speaking of sin, it might be helpful to remember that all sin is unhealthy, though certain sins may be more serious, since they move us further from him who is Light. 1 John 5:17 describes the situation in this way: "Every kind of wickedness is sin, but not all sin leads to death." In this context, that which leads to death may be equated with "mortal" while that which does not may be seen as "venial." The question may be better phrased by asking whether our life's actions are breaking or building our relationship with God, manifested by the way we relate to one another. If they are breaking our relationship, are they doing so in a deadly or mortal manner? Try not to get mired in useless speculations that weigh one mortal sin against thousands of venial sins. Such an approach misses the point and misconstrues the very nature of sin. In the *Rite of Penance* and the new *Code of Canon Law* (1983), serious or grave sin is the preferred term.

Remember also that the *Rite of Penance* emphasizes sin as an attitude or power rather than an act. One's "fundamental orientation of life" is seen as a guideline that situates sin in a perspective beyond individual acts. Note, for example, the Rite's Examination of Conscience (see chapter 6) in which the challenging question is "Where is my life really leading me?" By taking such an approach, the Church is striving to move us, her children, to the deeper understanding of grave (mortal) sin as a withdrawing from the communion of love with God—the God who desires to identify us as his children—through our withdrawal from the communion of love with others.

Q. Is the new Rite of Penance *meant to be used in all parishes?*
A. Promulgated in 1973, the new rite was to be implemented in all parishes in the United States by the First Sunday of Lent, 1977.

Q. Why must one perform a penance to be forgiven?

A. In the past, penance was viewed as necessary to pay the debt incurred by our sin. This was especially true during the Middle Ages, when penance was interpreted as providing "satisfaction" for one's sins. As the idea of satisfaction or payment developed, it became apparent that no one could "satisfy" through prayers or actions the number of sins committed. Such an approach would have taken more than a lifetime. Originally, penance was an *action* which externalized one's sincerity of repentance and shaped one's life to center on God.

More in line with this original understanding, acts of penance today are seen as the sign of the penitent's sincerity, and a focus indicating where a penitent's life is to change through his/her openness to the Spirit. An act of penance is not meant to be mere behavior modification, but the mystery of the Spirit's unfolding within the penitent, the liberating power of the Paschal Mystery.

Q. *When I go to the reconciliation room, do I have to go face to face to confess my sins?*
A. Every penitent has the option of celebrating the sacrament of reconciliation in the manner which makes him/her most comfortable. An individual can choose to kneel or sit behind a screen, or go face to face. Keep in mind, however, that an important gesture, namely, the laying on of hands, is not as well symbolized behind the screen.

Q. *As soon as I leave the reconciliation room, I begin to worry whether or not I confessed all my sins.*

The priest told me I was too scrupulous and should not worry about it. Despite his comments, I worry about it quite a bit. I even think, now, that my scrupulosity is a sin. Is it?

A.   Stating that scrupulosity is not a sin—it isn't—seldom relieves the individual from the pain of being scrupulous. When an individual encounters this particular inner attitude, it is important for him/her to realize its origin. Very often two threads woven together "create" the scrupulous person. The first thread might be viewed as a type of positive, namely, the person's deep desire to give everything to the Lord. Wanting more than anything else to be acceptable in the sight of God, the scrupulous person will probe his/her inner self with frightening deliberateness, looking for anything that may be a barrier to God's acceptance. This deliberateness begins, in its thoroughness, to assume the worst rather than the best. Everything, therefore, appears as an obstacle to God's love. Here is when it might be helpful for the individual penitent to remember the words of scripture which state that "nothing . . . will be able to come between us and the love of God" (Rm 8:38–39).

The second thread highlights the darker side of the fabric. This is the inner fear and anxiety that is often a part of the individual's life. The anxiety may be due to family difficulties, lack of a healthy self-image (remember that we are made in God's own image), or simply the type of personality that feeds on worry. The freedom of God's children is needed here, hence the Sacrament of Reconciliation, supported by regular prayer for inner healing, will often help the individual. Guidelines to follow: Pray for inner healing daily (see chapter 7 for explanation of such prayer) and celebrate the Sacrament of Reconciliation monthly. The individual should not be encouraged to celebrate the sacrament more frequently lest the scrupulosity be reinforced before the grace of the sacrament and the prayers for inner healing can have an effect.

Q.   When I go to celebrate the Sacrament of Reconciliation, should I seek spiritual direction or pastoral counseling at the same time?

A.   Although recent use often incorporates pastoral counseling and spiritual direction within the celebration of the sacrament, the practice remains questionable from several points of view. First of all, the celebration is a form of worship, not a form of therapy. Linking the two often encourages people to see the sacrament as a type of therapeutic purification set within a somewhat mechanical means of receiving grace.

This is not to say that counseling may not properly enter into the dialogue between the penitent and the priest (cf. the *Rite of Penance* 18, 44). In this context, however, the advice can seldom be broad or deep enough to serve as spiritual direction. In addition, one must not presume that the priest has the competency for counseling, or the charism for spiritual direction, neither of which are traditionally part of the charism called Holy Orders.

From a pastoral point of view, the individual person cannot be ignored if a need arises. Although the celebration of the sacrament may not be the best situation to receive counseling or spiritual direction, many people find it the only place they can receive help with their daily problems. Do not be offended if the priest asks you to see him at a later date within a different context, namely, the rectory office. This offer is being made so the best of both worlds can be received: the world of sacramental celebration and the world of spiritual direction or pastoral counseling. In all cases, the penitent's present need takes precedence over worship theories and ideals, provided it does not distort the presentation of the Father's healing love. An excellent treatment of this matter can be found in James Dallen's *The Reconciling Community* (New York: Pueblo Publishing Co., 1986), pp. 369f.

Notes

CHAPTER ONE

1. Richard M. Gula, *To Walk Together Again* (New York: Paulist Press, 1984), p. 188.

2. Gula, p. 192.

3. Raymond E. Brown, *The Gospel According to John*, The Anchor Bible, vol. 29A, pp. 1044–45.

4. Ladislas Orsy, *The Evolving Church and the Sacrament of Penance* (Denville, N.J.: Dimension Books, 1978), p. 29.

5. Orsy, p. 32. The list of serious sins, which were considered penance material, was not limited to three. Depending on the custom of each church, the list could have been longer.

6. Gula, p. 201.

7. Maria-Bruno Carra de Vaux Saint-Cyr, "The Sacrament of Penance: An Historical Outline," in *The Mystery of Sin and Forgiveness*, ed. Michael Taylor (New York: Alba House, 1971), p. 130.

8. Gula, p. 198.

9. Orsy, p. 34.

10. Gula, p. 201.

11. Maria-Bruno, pp. 141–45.

12. Maria-Bruno, p. 148.

13. Orsy, p. 44.

14. John T. McNeill and Helena M. Gamer, *Medieval Handbooks of Sin* (New York: Octagon Books, 1965), p. 251.

15. Gula, p. 211.

16. Maria-Bruno, p. 151.

17. Gula, p. 214.

18. Gula, p. 217.

19. Orsy, p. 123. This view is also maintained by Charles Curran in his work, "The Sacrament of Penance Today," *Contemporary Problems in Moral Theology* (Notre Dame: Fides Publisher, 1970), p. 160.

20. Orsy, p. 49.

21. Constitution on Divine Revelation, Dei Verbum, #8.

CHAPTER TWO

1. Augustine, *Enchiridion,* IX.

2. Augustine, *De Trinitate,* I, iv, 7.

3. This is based on the scholastic principle "omne agens agit sibi simili" that an effect is necessarily like its cause in some way and that to cause is per se to transmit a resemblance. Whatever proceeds from God, therefore, is in one sense the same as He, and in another sense different.

4. Raimundo Panikkar, *The Trinity and the Religious Experience of Man* (New York: Orbis Books, 1973), p. xi.

5. *De Trinitate,* VII, iv, 9; II, x, 18.

6. Bonaventure, *Breviloquium,* Part I, Chapter 3, Number 4.

7. Bonaventure, *Collationes in Hexaemeron,* I, 13.

8. Heribert Muhlen, *A Charismatic Theology,* tr. by Edward Quinn (New York: Paulist Press, 1978), p. 50.

9. Ewert H. Cousins, *Bonaventure and the Coincidence of Opposites* (Chicago: Franciscan Herald Press, 1977), p. 57, fn. 60.

10. Augustine, *Confessiones,* XIII, ix, 10.

11. *De Trinitate,* XV, xvii, 27; XV, xviii, 32.

12. *De Trinitate,* VII, iii, 5–6.

13. *Enchiridion,* XL.

14. *Hexaemeron,* IX, 2.

15. Zachary Hayes, *The Hidden Center* (New York: Paulist Press, 1981), p. 60.

16. Bonaventure, *Itinerarium,* II, 8.

17. Karl Rahner, "Experiencing the Spirit," in *The Practice of Faith,* ed. Karl Lehmann and Albert Raffelt (New York: Crossroads, 1983), pp. 82–84.

18. Rosemary Haughton, *The Passionate God* (New York: Paulist Press, 1981).

19. Franz Jozef van Beeck, S.J., *Christ Proclaimed: Christology as Rhetoric* (New York: Paulist Press, 1979), p. 422.

20. For a complete explanation of these terms, see Sabbas J. Kilian, "The Holy Spirit in Christ and in Christians," *The American Benedictine Review* 20, (March 1969).

21. Muhlen, p. 39.

22. John Shea, *The Experience Called Spirit* (Chicago: Thomas More Press, 1983), p. 153. One might say that this desire opens one up to the ultimate cause of desire, who is also the only one who can fulfill the desire, namely, Love.

23. Karl Rahner, *A Rahner Reader* (New York: Seabury

Press, 1975), p. 20. Interestingly enough, this yearning stirs within the audacious desire that God surrender himself to us, which Jesus comes to show has already been done.

24. This is supported throughout John of the Cross's *Spiritual Canticle*, tr. E. Allison Peers (New York: Doubleday Image Books, 1961). Compare, for example, stanza 39.6: "Whereas souls possess these same blessings by participation as He possesses by nature; for the which cause they are truly gods by participation, equals of God and His companions."

25. Augustine, Sermon #34, 1–3, 5–6; CCL 41, 424–426.

26. Aelred Squire, *Asking the Fathers* (New York: Morehouse-Barlow, 1973), p. 19.

27. Shea, cf. Chapter 4.

28. Bernard Cooke, *Sacraments and Sacramentality* (Mystic, Conn.: Twenty-Third Publications, 1983), p. 199.

29. David O'Rourke, *A Process Called Conversion* (Garden City, N.Y.: Doubleday & Company, 1985), p. 51.

30. O'Rourke, pp. 51–52.

31. O'Rourke, p. 170.

32. O'Rourke, p. 173.

33. O'Rourke, p. 188.

34. Dag Hammarskjöld, *Markings*, tr. by Leif Sjöberg and W. H. Auden (New York: Alfred A. Knopf, 1968), p. 197.

35. James Dallen, *The Reconciling Community* (New York: Pueblo Publishing Co., 1986), p. 261.

36. Cooke, p. 199.

37. Dallen, p. 267.

38. Cooke, p. 212.

CHAPTER THREE

1. *Sacrosanctum Concilium*, no. 72: AAS 56 (1964) 118.

2. In *Sacramentum Paenitentiae*, VII (June 16, 1972), the Sacred Congregation for the Doctrine of the Faith issued the following directive: "Unless there is a good reason preventing it, those who receive pardon for serious sin through general absolution are to go to auricular confession before any further reception of general absolution. And unless a moral impossibility stands in the way, they are absolutely bound to go to a confessor within one year. For the precept binding every one of the faithful binds them as well, namely, to confess individually to a priest at least once a year all those grave sins not hitherto confessed one by one." Note that this exhortation echoes Canon 989 which

applies to those guilty of serious sins, namely, "After having attained the age of discretion, each of the faithful is bound by an obligation faithfully to confess serious sins at least once a year."

3. *Rite of Penance,* 6c, in "The Rites of the Catholic Church" (New York: Pueblo Publishing Co., 1976).

CHAPTER FOUR

1. Ladislas Orsy, *The Evolving Church and the Sacrament of Penance* (Denville, N.J.: Dimension Books, 1978), p. 132.

2. Orsy, p. 141.

3. M. Francis Mannion, *Worship,* Vol. 60, No. 2 (March 1986): 104.

4. Mannion, p. 109.

5. Mannion, p. 108.

6. Orsy, p. 155.

7. Orsy maintains (p. 146) that "it is a sound principle of interpretation in canon law that whenever there is a favor granted, it must be interpreted broadly." The power to absolve is a favor, hence it should be interpreted broadly.

8. Ladislas Orsy, *Theological Studies,* Vol. 45, No. 4 (December 1984): 685.

9. Orsy, *Theological Studies,* p. 679. On the same page is an important, though technical, text: "The message of the canon sounds clear enough: no such intention, no absolution. But how can anyone ascertain its presence in the minds and hearts of the people? Could such determination be virtual, habitual, interpretative, or must it be actual? Could it be implicit (not thought of), or must it be explicit (in the mind)—to use some of the technical distinctions? . . . Does it follow that when, under the pressure of circumstances, it occurs to no one to think or to speak of the intention, the absolution is invalid?"

10. Orsy, *Theological Studies,* p. 682.

11. *Rite of Penance,* 4.

12. Matthew and Dennis Linn, *Healing of Memories* (Ramsey, N.J.: Paulist Press, 1974); Barbara Shlemon, *Healing Prayer* (Notre Dame: Ave Maria Press, 1976); Michael Scanlan, *The Power in Penance* (Notre Dame: Ave Maria Press, 1972); Michael Scanlan, *Inner Healing* (Ramsey, N.J.: Paulist Press, 1974). These are some of the texts that delve more deeply into the experience of inner healing.

OTHER IMAGE BOOKS

OTHER IMAGE BOOKS